*The Old Testament
in Christian Preaching*

THE OLD TESTAMENT IN CHRISTIAN PREACHING

by

Lawrence E. Toombs

Philadelphia

THE WESTMINSTER PRESS

LIBRARY OF CONGRESS CATALOG CARD No. 61-11635

PRINTED IN THE UNITED STATES OF AMERICA

Contents

Preface

With the great activity currently taking place in the field of Old Testament studies it is difficult to imagine a gap in the literature. Yet one — and a serious one at that — exists at the point of communicating the results of Old Testament scholarship in a manner sympathetic to, and directed toward, the preacher and his task. There is no scarcity of " sermon hearts," or even of full-length sermons, based on the Old Testament, but these are as likely to muddy the waters as to clarify them. If a preacher is content to be a purveyor at second hand of the thoughts of other men, he may be satisfied with " canned " sermons, and if he is imaginative, he may profit by them as examples for his own preaching. But the real preaching need is a firsthand knowledge of and affection for the Old Testament, a consciousness that it contains a homiletic richness that is rarely presented from the pulpit, and a willingness to work at Old Testament study in order to bring this latent wealth to light.

This book is intended to help the preacher fulfill this part of his office. It attempts first to set the Old Testament in a relationship to the New which will be productive of valuable results in the Christian pulpit. It then proceeds to outline some of the principal characteristics of Old Testament thought and the bearing of these on the preacher's task. The body of the book is taken up with a review of the principal Old Testament themes: the covenant, the promise to the fathers, the Fall of mankind, the prophetic movement and the message of the prophets, and finally, the piety of the psalmists.

Inevitably many themes dear to the heart of the preacher are left out, notably the fifty-third chapter of Isaiah and The Book of Job. The justification, if one can be made, of these omissions is that the presentation is intended to provide a typical treatment of selected material, and to offer a method and point of view by which the rest of the material may be studied.

This book has been provided with a topical index so that it may serve to some degree as a reference work when the preacher needs to locate quickly the treatment of a particular topic or passage.

While the primary emphasis of this book is on the preaching of the Old Testament in the context of New Testament faith, it is hoped that it may also have some usefulness in the guidance of adult classes in the church school or of classes preparatory to church membership. It may even be of some interest to the layman who is pondering the question, Why does the Christian church retain the Old Testament in its Scriptures?

The thankless but invaluable task of preparing the index was done by my wife, and to her my best thanks. For the rest, acknowledgments of further indebtedness would fill volumes. Teachers, students, scholars, and writers on the Old Testament have all contributed to the author's own

thought, and if he does not directly acknowledge his indebtedness by footnotes, the charitable reader will attribute his
negligence to unwillingness to involve them in his errors.

LAWRENCE E. TOOMBS

Madison, New Jersey

I

The Old Testament and Christian Preaching

Biblical scholars often look with condescension on the preacher, regarding him as a mere sermonizer who lacks the specialist's training necessary to make him a reliable interpreter of Scripture. Too often the preacher surrenders to this judgment, and admitting himself to be unqualified, concludes that he ought to avoid further criticism by not attempting serious Biblical interpretation from the pulpit. There is often a trace of resentment in the preacher's reaction. The work of the scholars is, he thinks, too erudite to be of much use in the pulpit, and in any event quite irrelevant to the modern scene against which the sermon must be spoken and heard. The scholar goes on his way writing books for his pupils and for other scholars; and the minister marches resolutely on his, satisfied with little homilies on how to live decently, or with analyses, some acute and some banal, of the social, political, and psychological scene of the present day, which because they deal with current topics he has deluded himself into thinking are relevant. In this divorce between the study and the pulpit, the ordinary Christian is the loser. He is being robbed of his right to hear the Word of God faithfully expounded.

In the interpretation of the Scripture within the framework of the church, the pastor is the indispensable man. Protestant tradition gives a high place to the Bible as the principal channel of divine grace by which the power of the eternal God is brought into saving contact with the sin and need of mankind. The position of the parish minister in this tradition is fairly expressed by the second vow taken by Methodists at their ordination as elder: " Are you persuaded that the Holy Scriptures contain all truth required for eternal salvation through faith in Jesus Christ? And are you determined out of the same Holy Scriptures so to instruct the people committed to your charge that they may enter into eternal life? " These words express a vital and urgent task in which the whole mission of the church is at stake.

The Bible was not written to be studied dispassionately, as one studies mathematical theory. Its very nature as witness to the saving revelation of God requires that its message be heard by everyone who can be prevailed upon to listen. In other words, the Bible was made to be preached. The minister may not have the specialist's technical knowledge, but he reaches the persons for whom the Scripture was intended. His role is therefore more vital than that of the Biblical scholar. When he stands up to preach, no teacher can take his place, for he is proclaiming the Word of God to the people.

These are the convictions that motivated the writing of this book. It does not intend to dispense " canned " sermons on Biblical themes. Rather, it follows loosely the outline of what is called " Old Testament Introduction," bringing out, as it goes along, the homiletic possibilities of the discoveries that scholars have made about the literary nature and archaeological background of the Old Testament. The material contained in the book is, however, pulpit-tested. The author has himself preached every major theme found in these pages, and the italicized headings give in a general way the main points of these sermons or include the idea on which the sermon was based. The aim of the book is simple: to open up to the preacher, and through him to the congregation, some of the many possibilities which the Old Testament contains for a deeper understanding of the Christian gospel.

THE NATURE OF BIBLICAL PREACHING

Biblical preaching does not consist in having a text and preaching a sermon, two operations that may be nearly unrelated to one another. It consists in determining the *intention* of the passage to be preached, and then taking up that intent, looking at it from various points of view and applying it in various ways until it takes on clarity and meaning in the minds of the hearers. When the sermon is over, it does not matter if the hearers remember what the preacher has said as long as they retain in their minds the Scripture that was preached. The sincerest compliment a preacher can receive is not, " I enjoyed the sermon," but " I never understood that Scripture as well before." The preacher is perpetually in the position of Second Isaiah, preparing the way of the Lord. His task is to clarify the Scripture so that the living Word of God may do its own work in the hearts of the congregation.

To prepare a sermon that will do this involves four necessary stages. These may, for convenience, be called: (1) the text, (2) the context, (3) the revelation, and (4) the application.

1. *The Text*. Persons who know the original languages can go directly to the Greek and Hebrew texts, and with the aid of lexicon and critical notes examine the words and their meanings at first hand. For those who do not know the languages, a wide variety of translations, paraphrases, and commentaries are available. These should be diligently compared with one another in order to discover the various shades of meaning that the original intended to convey. Why is this particular word chosen and no other? Why is it used in this specific place? Such poring over the Scriptures is a time-consuming process, and many ministers regard it as a bad investment of precious hours. But time could hardly be better spent. The words of the Bible, especially in familiar passages, have a tendency to skip off the surface of the mind like flat stones off water unless some device is deliberately used to force attention to each significant word.

Most readers of the Twenty-third Psalm see in it only the comfort and consolation that it offers. The congregation sits in blissful self-congratulation while the minister repeats, " The Lord is my shepherd, I shall not want," never realizing that the psalm is a confession of the sheeplike nature of the worshipers, ornery and self-willed creatures who could not live a week in the rigors of the wilderness without the constant care and guidance of the shepherd. When looked at closely, the psalm is more than a guarantee of unlimited blessing. It is a confession of complete dependence on God. Such a meaning in Biblical passages always escapes the casual reader.

2. *The Context*. Once the passage is understood, the question becomes, " What did it mean to those who first heard it spoken or read? " A twofold context is involved in this question. The narrower setting of the passage in the piece of

literature of which it is a part must be explored. For example, the story of the Tower of Babel can be understood in its full force only when seen as part of the insight into human nature possessed by the first and possibly the greatest of Israel's theologians, the unknown genius to whom scholarship has given the depressing name "the Yahwist" (see Chapter IV).

In a wider sense the context of a passage is the whole cultural, historical, and religious situation existing at the time the passage originated. The familiar line of the First Psalm offers a homely example:

> The wicked are not so,
>   but are like chaff which the wind drives away.
> (V. 4.)

It presupposes a knowledge of the ancient process of threshing grain. In vivid metaphor the psalmist is describing the inability of wickedness to stand the pressures and winds of life, the instability and impermanence of evil, and the absence in it of any genuine nourishment for human life. It would be an unimaginative minister who could not construct a sermon from those three points, unified as they are in the pictorial image of the threshing floor.

3. *The Revelation.* Thus far the preparation of the sermon has been straightforward and objective, not involving the personality and convictions of the preacher. When, however, the question of the revelation involved in the Scripture is raised, the problem becomes at once more subjective and more difficult. If we had to deal with each passage separately, drawing from it a variety of unrelated moral and religious teachings, the task would be impossible. But we are not compelled to deal with the Bible in this piecemeal fashion. The prophetic movement has left us a clear guide to the

proper starting point and method of approach to all Biblical passages.

The prophet began his thought with God, not with man. He proceeded from what he knew of God to what he would say about the condition and needs of men. This prophetic method constitutes a profound homiletical principle. The starting point of a sermon is what God has revealed himself to be; and the human being with his hopes and fears, his dreads, follies, and dreams, is seen in the light of the self-revelation of God. This is a reflection of the truth expressed in the Priestly Creation story, " God created man in his own image " (Gen. 1:27). The preacher has no right to turn this around and make God in the image of man. He must continually ask himself what the Scripture on which he intends to preach says about the character and activity of God. When he has answered that question, he is at the place where the sermon ought to begin.

Many magnificent Old Testament passages are consistently misrepresented because of failure to recognize that the nature of God is their true starting point. The concluding words of Isa., ch. 40, are often broken off from their context, and quoted in isolation:

> They who wait for the Lord shall renew
>   their strength,
>   they shall mount up with wings like eagles,
> they shall run and not be weary,
>   they shall walk and not faint.
>
> (V. 31.)

So used, the passage may be read as a panegyric on the powers latent in man and taken to mean that, with a little help from God, human nature may enter the eaglelike existence.

The passage begins properly with v. 28, and, taken as a whole, vigorously contrasts the unlimited nature of God with the space- and time-bound life of man. The prophet picks up one by one the facts of human existence which remind a man that in spite of his pretensions to greatness he is in the grip of forces over which he has no control: time, which makes him the servant of the clock and in the end wears him out and kills him; space, which, all his rockets and jet aircraft notwithstanding, confines him to a tiny corner of the universe; fatigue, which cuts off his most conscientious efforts and sends him to bed with the great thought unformed and the great deed undone; limited knowledge, which puts him in the unhappy position of raising ten questions for every one he is able to solve. None of these things, which write question marks over human existence, have any power to bind or limit the majestic God of the prophet.

> The Lord is the everlasting God [unlimited by time],
>   the Creator of the ends of the earth [sovereign over space].
> He does not faint or grow weary [impervious to fatigue],
>   his understanding is unsearchable [free of error].
>
> (V. 28.)

If the prophet went no farther, his theology would be mere mockery of the human state, an open invitation to despair. But the prophet's God is not sheer majesty. He is also a God of mercy. Out of the abundance of his divine nature he is ready to bestow something of himself upon his human creatures, and his strength overflows to men.

He gives power to the faint,
and to him who has no might he increases
strength.

(V. 29.)

The prophet is sure that victorious living is possible only
by accepting the divine gift. Let even the most gifted and
capable of human beings, the youth (Hebrew, *bāḥūr,* " the
choice one "), with all his powers fresh within him, set out
to conquer the world in his own strength and he will inevitably fail. The beginning may be promising enough —
hat on the side of his head, and the world his oyster — but
the end is the long, shuddering fall of complete exhaustion,
when the human powers are used up and there is no reser-
voir from which renewal may come.

Even youths shall faint and be weary,
and young men shall fall exhausted.

(V. 30.)

All life ends in frustration and despair except that which
is grounded in steadfast allegiance to " the everlasting God."
In this relationship, which the prophet calls " waiting for
the Lord," a miracle takes place. Man shares in the life of
God, and his human powers are lifted to new and unsuspected heights. " They shall mount up with wings like
eagles."

The eagle metaphor is worth looking at more closely.
Sweeping and soaring over the plain, the eagle is the very
epitome of freedom. To the earth-bound human below, the
eagle seems to have shaken off the bonds of gravity. But
seen at closer range, the eagle's wings are strained against
the air in which he moves, every feather set to catch its
slightest movement. He continues to fly only so long as he
is sensitive and obedient to the air around him. He is free

of the earth because he has become the servant of a new element. Christian liberty is like the eagle's flight, free of the demands and tensions of the world because submitted to the new demands and tensions of being " in Christ " (see Gal. 6:11-16).

The detailed exegesis of Isa. 40:28-31 illustrates how the revelatory elements of a Biblical passage may be exposed by beginning where the prophet himself began with his insight into the character of God, and by following the prophet's own line of development until it brings us face to face with Jesus Christ.

4. *The Application.* With the text, context, and revelatory quality of the Scripture in his mind, the preacher is now ready to apply its message to the specific concerns of the congregation. Any sooner is too soon. The topsy-turvy procedure of deciding first the message to be brought to the congregation and then searching out a text or two that appear to fit is futile and self-defeating. The sermon may be clever and even helpful, but it will be the minister's mind and the minister's wisdom that the congregation encounters. And these are mighty poor substitutes for the Word of God.

How the application is made cannot be determined in advance. Its structure must arise out of the minister's pastoral experience. He knows his congregation, the problems they face and the temptations that press upon them. All the wisdom provided by his parish work and all his knowledge of the contemporary world are brought to bear on the Scripture. But they are used now to interpret the Word, not to distort and falsify the Word. In this way the Scripture may speak to the contemporary mind. The contemporary mind will not be allowed to come to the Bible, as to a mirror, looking for flattering reflections of itself.

THE OLD TESTAMENT AND THE NEW

The Christian minister does not preach the Old Testament, in the sense that his sermon arises out of and is confined to that section of the Bible. His preaching is centered in the gospel, and issues in a distinctively Christian message. This fact faces the Christian preacher with many dilemmas and questions. Can he ignore the Old Testament, and confine himself entirely to the New? Can he use the Old Testament in a Christian setting without distorting its original meaning and forcing it to say what he wishes it to say? Must he confine himself to a small circle of " old reliables," such as Ps. 23 and Isa., ch. 53, which are universally recognized as significant preparations for the gospel? What relevance has the story of Israel, from her beginnings in the wilderness of Sinai to her end under the iron heel of Rome, to the appearance in history of God made flesh to dwell with men? Each of these questions depends for its answer on one underlying problem, that of the relationship between the Old and the New Testaments.

Every Christian thinker of any stature has puzzled over the twofold nature of his sacred Book. Emil G. Kraeling, in his work *The Old Testament Since the Reformation* (Harper & Brothers, 1955), summarizes the solutions offered from Luther to Bultmann, and although it is a masterpiece of condensation, the book runs to 320 pages. Through this maze of varying opinion and speculation the minister must find his way to an answer, for whether or not he has thought seriously about the problem, every sermon he preaches implies an answer. The only option is whether the solution will be thoughtful and sincere, or haphazard and careless. A thorough discussion of so complex a problem is beyond the scope of this book, but the question of the relationship between the Old and New Testaments is so central to the preacher's task that the main lines of current discussion should at least be sketched.

The Revised Standard Version bears the full title, *The Holy Bible, Containing the Old and New Testaments*. The very wording raises the question of relationship. Where shall the emphasis be placed? On the unity that exists between the two divisions of the Bible because they are both testaments? Or on the radical difference between them in that one is old and the other new?

Modern fundamentalism reduces the difference between the Testaments almost to the vanishing point. The two stand on the same level of inspiration. Every sentence of the Old Testament is a direct word from God, and since God's Word is timeless, every part of the Old Testament is equally the Word to the twentieth century. While this view has the apparent virtue of simplicity, it cannot be successfully maintained in the practice of preaching. Its most vigorous supporter would scarcely preach with the same fervor and conviction on " You shall not sow your field with two kinds of seed " as on " You shall love your neighbor as yourself." Yet the passages are found in two consecutive verses in Leviticus (ch. 19:18-19).

Some scholars at the opposite pole from fundamentalism emphasize the difference between the Testaments to such a degree that their unity vanishes. The Old is cultic, centered in the priesthood and the Temple ritual. The New bursts free of the cultic pattern and sees its whole meaning fulfilled in the person of Christ. The Old is national, bound to a specific nation in its geographic homeland. The New is transnational, a gospel for the whole world. The Old is " of the earth earthy," confined to this side of death. The New looks beyond the grave to the hope of an eternal life in which death is swallowed up in victory. The Old is the book of the wrath of God. The New is the record of his grace. The Old is all law; the New, all gospel. Such a portrait in black and white has great preaching power. It makes the Old Testament serve Christian self-understanding by displaying Christianity's diametric opposite. It proclaims the radically new thing that God has done for man in Jesus Christ, and shows the Christian the rock from whence he was hewn. The formula of absolute contrast may, however, become too narrowly confining to do justice to the truth of either Testament. Hosea's magnificent wrestling with the loving-kindness of God, Jeremiah's agonizing search for the inner meaning of " covenant," Second Isaiah's concept of the Suffering Servant of the Lord cannot be put into the strait jacket of a complete cleavage between the Testaments.

The method of holding the two Testaments together most in vogue in modern Biblical scholarship uses the category of history. From the secular historian's point of view it is a plain fact that Christianity is a development out of postexilic Judaism, and that there is a demonstrable continuity between Moses and Christ. But the answer to the larger question, What, if anything, does this continuity mean theologically? is not so obvious. It is possible to see in the historical events a record of man's eternal questing after the higher and the nobler. The Old Testament then becomes the book of Israel's search for God, and its pages display the evolution of her religious ideas from low to high, from primitive to developed, until they reach their climax in the greatest religious teacher of them all, Jesus of Nazareth. From the Biblical point of view, this reading of the Scriptures as the story of man's upward progress in religious insight is a dangerous lie. It puts man and his deeds at the center of the theological universe where only God can be allowed to stand.

It denies by implication the uniqueness of the Biblical revelation, and indeed calls in question the very idea of revelation. And it opens a wide door to the practitioners of cults of self-improvement and self-salvation.

The Biblical history may, however, be read as a record of God's quest for fallen man, and his outreach to humanity through his saving acts in history. The two pivotal events in the story of God's delivering deeds are the exodus from Egypt and the event of Christ. Israel's history thus becomes *Heilsgeschichte,* salvation history, moving toward the conclusive act of salvation in Jesus Christ, or "progressive revelation," leading on to the perfect revelation in Christ of God's nature and purpose.

The Old and New Testaments may be kept together theologically by other means than the category of history. The Christian preacher cannot but be attracted by the forthright declaration of Otto Procksch, "*Alle Theologie ist Christologie.*" If all theology is Christology, the unity between the Testaments must be provided by the figure of Christ himself. The Old Testament is the witness to Christ, the promise, the prophecy, and the preparation of which the incarnation is the realization and fulfillment. The key to the meaning of the Old Testament and the reason it is necessary to the Christian church is its prevision and foreshadowing of Christ. Impressive as this is, the Christocentric interpretation of the Old Testament, when followed exclusively and in isolation from alternative views, leaves the way clear for gross extravagances of exegesis in which allegorical imagination, uncontrolled by historical discipline, discovers Christ in unlikely or impossible places in the Old Testament.

Paul taught the Christian church that its lifeblood is faith. Perhaps, then, faith is the only cement that can hold the Testaments together for the Christian. The Christian is what

he is because of a personal encounter in the living present
with the living Christ, in which he has received the forgiving grace of God. The words of the Old Testament were not
spoken directly to such a person. Jeremiah, for example,
proclaimed a message from God to a theocratic state trem-
bling on the edge of extinction before the armies of Babylon.
What can his words mean to a man in Christ? Has their
validity perished along with the historical and political setting which first called them forth? Not necessarily, for the
old covenant is founded on an understanding of human
existence which is also basic to the gospel. It sees man, the
creature of God and living under the divine command, yet a
rebel against God's demand for obedience. It perceives the
profound human need for the forgiveness and grace of God,
if man is to escape from the threat of death under which his
rebellion has placed him. It contrasts faithless man with the
eternally faithful God. Christian faith takes the Old Testament words that were addressed to others and hears them
spoken to itself. The Christian holds the Old Testament up
as a mirror and sees in its understanding of the human predicament the reflection of his own face. He says of the Old
Testament, " It is the story of my life." He does this not by
fact but by faith, and by faith alone.

Although the preaching minister's answer to the question
of the relationship between the Testaments may not differ
in essentials from that of the theologian, it is governed by
three conditions arising out of the preacher's special office as
herald of the Word of God.

1. The preacher must be able to take his stand squarely
in the New Testament faith, so that, although he may preach
from the Old Testament, he will never be preaching the Old
Testament, but always his own distinctive Christian gospel.
In other words, the preacher's stance must always be Christo-

centric, rooted and grounded in the faith he is called to declare.

2. At the same time, the preacher must not fall into the error of treating the Old and New Testaments as if they were on the same level of inspiration and insight. Between Malachi and Matthew something transformingly new took place, and in that new thing the old passed away. The unity of the Testaments cannot be allowed to mask the tensions and fundamental differences that exist between them.

3. The preacher's understanding of the relationship between the Testaments must be serviceable to him as a guide in the composition and construction of his sermons. "True in theory, but unworkable in practice" is a fallacy that operates too often to divorce the study from the pulpit. A sound theology will give a sermon not only content and power but form and structure as well.

These conditions are best met by seeing the Old Testament related to the New as hope to fulfillment, as question to answer, as suggestion to reality.

Hope and Fulfillment. Seen through Christian eyes, the Old Testament is an incomplete book. Repeatedly it points beyond itself to something still to come. Longings, hopes, and aspirations are raised, but never fulfilled. Promises are made, but not realized. The vision is seen in a glass dimly, with the expectation that someday it may be face to face. The prophets often express this mood of unfulfilled hope in such sentences as, "The Lord will have compassion on Jacob" (Isa. 14:1), and "Behold, the days are coming" (Jer. 9:25; 23:5). These are not so much predictions as expressions of a longing so intense that it leaps beyond itself into the future. The great moment to which the Old Testament looks forward is the coming of Christ, in whom its hopes are fulfilled and its promises realized. By showing his people the character of the hope, the minister may give new vividness and clarity to the nature of the realization.

Jeremiah's new covenant (ch. 31:31-34) is the direct expression of such hope looking to the future for its fulfillment. " The days are coming when I will make a new covenant with the house of Israel and the house of Judah." (V. 31.)

The obvious difference between the new covenant and the old is that its law will become a part of the inner nature of the covenant people written " not on tablets of stone " (II Cor. 3:3). The formalized, codified law, whether it be the Constitution of the United States or the Holy Bible, can easily be treated as a thing to be examined, studied, and even revered, without being made an *operative* part of life. Legalistic adherence to the Constitution, or " bibliolatry " in which the Bible becomes a fetish, the living spirit being lost but the words remaining all important, are the inevitable result. Jeremiah's new covenant is, therefore, a hope-filled looking forward to the revelation in Christ in which the law is transcended altogether, and the operation of the Spirit of Christ within the believer becomes the motivating power of the Christian life (II Cor. 3:17).

The element of genuine novelty in the new covenant resides, not in this inwardness that was already foreshadowed in Deut. 30:11-14, but in the climax of Jeremiah's oracle, " I will forgive their iniquity, and I will remember their sin no more " (ch. 31:34). The covenant of Sinai, which first brought Israel and her God together, was a covenant of grace, founded on the unearned deliverance from Egyptian slavery (see Chapter III). The law was given in the context of this deliverance, and was accepted in gratitude as governing Israel's national life. This old covenant presented a portrait in black and white. Obedience meant life; disobedience, judgment and death (Deut. 30:15). No word was said of forgiveness. Until the law had been accepted and broken, the need of radical forgiveness could hardly have been felt. After the social and religious degeneration of the seventh and eighth centuries B.C. it became evident that, if the covenant bond was to be restored, divine grace would have to take a new and deeper form. Deliverance from political enemies was no longer sufficient. God's loving-kindness must deal with the rebellious spirit that had broken the covenant bond. Therefore the essence of the new covenant is grace operating as forgiveness.

Jeremiah here genuinely looks toward the New Testament. His covenant of forgiveness is the promise of that gospel of which reconciliation is the keynote, and gives the Christian preacher an Old Testament entree into New Testament faith.

In his great oracle on the sustaining power of God, Second Isaiah offers another familiar example of the hope-fulfillment theme (Isa. 55:1-5). God's love is as universal as mankind's thirst for him, and is poured out generously and freely to satisfy his need (v. 1). To come to these waters and eat of this bread is an unfailing protection against false saviors who offer only dry and tasteless Dead Sea fruit (v. 2). In these declarations about God and man, the prophet has opened windows through which the Christian preacher can let his congregation see the work of Christ.

Once alerted to the hope-fulfillment relationship between the Testaments, the preacher will detect many passages in which the hope is indirect or implied. A sentence such as, "Where there is no prophecy the people cast off restraint" has positive and negative implications. The willfulness and self-destructive quality of a life for which the will of God is not known and does not matter, and the corresponding necessity of the speaking and hearing of God's word if life is to have strength and meaning, point beyond the Old Testament insight to the proclamation of the will of God in the ministry of Christ, where simultaneously prophecy reaches its fulfillment and the people put on the restraint of Christ in which alone genuine liberty is to be found (II Cor. 5:14).

Question and Answer. This category of relationship between the Testaments is a minor variation of the hope-fulfillment theme, made desirable by the fact that the Old Testament is often found in the interrogative mood. Three examples may illustrate the principle.

"If a man die, shall he live again?" (Job 14:14.) The question arises in the lowest depths of Job's suffering. He sees, around the stump of a felled tree, the miracle of reviving life as new green shoots push up from the old root. For a moment he feels that in man also, new life might be born in the body cut down by death. If he could believe this, he might have hope even in his suffering. But such faith is impossible for him.

> Man dies, and is laid low;
> Man breathes his last, and where is he?
> (Job 14:10.)

The Christian preacher cannot take it for granted that the gospel of eternal life is accepted immediately and unquestioningly by his congregation. Job is not alone in his desperate desire for life beyond death, nor in putting it aside as illusion. Both the longing and the doubt must be seriously dealt with, not impatiently rejected as heretical. The Christian assurance of immortality is more honestly preached if it is placed in the setting of Job's predicament and his question.

"Where shall wisdom be found?" (Job 28:12.) The remarkable hymn to wisdom in Job, ch. 28, describes the splendid achievements of human skill; the mines that find the raw ore beneath the ground (vs. 1-6), the rock-cut tunnels of the engineers (vs. 9-10), and the dams that check the flow of mighty rivers (v. 11). But technical knowledge is not wisdom. In spite of his know-how, wisdom still eludes man. It cannot be acquired by skill or bought with money (vs. 12-19). Wisdom is the possession of God alone, and if it comes to man, it comes only to him who recognizes his helplessness to make himself wise and is ready in humble reverence to seek his wisdom as a gift of God. "The fear of the Lord, that is wisdom." (V. 28.) The insistence that wisdom is a gift of God to those of humble and reverent spirit is the proper prolegomenon to the preaching of Christ as the "wisdom of God" (I Cor. 1:18-30).

"Should such a man as I flee?" (Neh. 6:11.) This question might mistakenly be regarded as a Biblical echo of the defiant spirit of William Ernest Henley's lines:

> Under the bludgeonings of chance
> My head is bloody, but unbowed.

Nehemiah is not, however, pitting his single life against the world simply for the sake of proving his own inflexibility. He came to Jerusalem under the call of God, with a task to do. Such a man, called and commissioned by God, will not run because some prince rattles a saber at him. From the Christian pulpit a call to courage and steadfastness based on Nehemiah's question must center in Christ, but the principle involved is the same. The consciousness of being called by Christ and commissioned to witness to his gospel is the authentic source of Christian steadfastness. Such a man will not flee.

In the background of specific questions such as those discussed above is the one important question which the Old Testament as a whole asks. Having reached an understanding of the nature of man and a vision of the character of God unattained in any other religion, and having seen its vision disappointed and broken on the rock of historic fact, the Old Testament demands to know whether these things are idle dreams or whether they can find their fulfillment. The New Testament replies that they can, and have. The Christian preacher holds all his homiletic use of the lesser questions within the spirit of this larger one.

Suggestion and Reality. The narrative parts of the Old Testament contain a relatively unexplored mine of homiletic possibilities. These sections of the Scripture dealing with " old, unhappy, far-off things, and battles long ago," apparently have little relevance to contemporary life, and can serve a homiletic purpose only by distortion of their original meaning. But the method indicated here, and called " suggestion and reality," allows some of this material to be brought into use.

It is easier to illustrate than to describe the method. When David, hard driven by his rebellious son Absalom, fled from Jerusalem, he stood by the brook Kidron to watch his loyal followers march from the city to join him in exile (II Sam. 15:13-23). The king was surprised to see among them the plumed helmets of Philistine warriors, and to recognize at their head one of his ablest soldiers, the captain of the Philistine mercenaries, Ittai of Gath.

" Why do you also go with us, . . . for you are a foreigner? " the king asks.

Ittai replies, "As the Lord lives, and as my lord the king lives, wherever my lord the king shall be, whether for death or for life, there also will your servant be."

The suggestion of the passage is the absolute devotion of the warrior to the king he loves. The reality to which it points is the devotion, come life or death, of the Christian to his heavenly King and Lord.

The danger of allegorizing the text is apparent, and is always present in the use of the suggestion-reality theme. When the preacher begins, for example, to detect in Ittai's foreign birth a promise of the conversion of the Gentiles, or to see a parallel between David's exile and the temptations of Christ he is caught in the web of allegory. Nevertheless, with proper controls the principle of suggestion and reality can bring to life many dead passages in the Old Testament, and in particular in the historic books.

The suggestion must fall within the range of metaphors applied by the Old Testament itself to the relationship between God and man. The story of Ittai deals on a high level with the king-subject relationship, one of the most pervasive of Old Testament metaphors. It expresses the loyalty which marks that relationship at its human best; and therefore offers a legitimate suggestion of the ultimate loyalty due to the sovereign God.

In a similar way, David's agonized cry over the death of his rebellious son, Absalom (II Sam. 18:33), is a human suggestion of the agony in the heart of God when his love is rejected by his disobedient children. The father-son relationship, from which this suggestion is drawn, obviously belongs among the metaphors endorsed by the Old Testament.

A study of the Biblical narratives will reveal many other such suggestions, the use of which will lend color and life to the presentation of the gospel. The minister need never go beyond the Bible for his illustrations. The tree and the stream, the eagle and the eaglet, the sheltering rock and the weary traveler, the shepherd and his sheep, provide suggestions in plenty by means of which he may bear witness to the truth of the gospel. The theological justification of the method and other examples of its use will be found in Chapter II.

THE DIFFERENCE BETWEEN THE OLD AND THE NEW

The two Testaments are not directly equivalent to each other. The fulfillment is never precisely the same as the hope, the answer often changes the question, and the reality is always greater than the suggestion can contain. The preacher must therefore be mindful that he does not gloss over the crucial differences between the two parts of his Scripture.

In the first place the center is different in the two documents. The great themes of the old covenant — righteousness, truth, forgiveness, salvation, peace, joy — are related to the work of Christ, and in the change some themes are lost altogether. The vindictive cry for vengeance against the enemies of Israel disappears altogether in the command to love. The institutions of blood sacrifice and the Day of Atonement are so taken up in the work of Christ that they disappear as living elements in the ritual. However, their disappearance and the reasons for it are highly instructive to the preacher.

The shift of center means a basic change in the nature of the religious community in the two Testaments. The Old is fundamentally national. Its revelation is for a people joined by the natural ties of race and living in definable geographic boundaries. The doctrine of the remnant, the faithful Israel within rebellious Israel, narrows rather than widens the scope of the community. In sharpest contrast the New Testament church cuts across all boundaries of race, social status, and geography, becoming international, or, better, transnational.

This transformation in the nature of the community has important consequences. War, accepted in the Old Testament as a proper business for the state and raised to sacred status in the theology of the " Holy War," was impossible to the church. There were no enemies for the transnational community to fight except the universal enemies of the human spirit. Accordingly, the vocabulary of the Holy War was adapted to the struggle against the forces of evil. The ideal of the brotherhood by birth was transmuted into brotherhood in Christ, and the role of the Messiah was recast to fit the new international outlook. Thus, the Messianic prophecies of the Old Testament are not *literally* fulfilled. They are reread and reinterpreted in the light of the fact of Christ.

The minister is faced with a dilemma which comes to an acute point in the Old Testament social ethics. He cannot simply apply these ethics to any modern state, and demand that the nation behave according to the law of ancient Israel. Ancient Israel was a theocracy, deriving its law in theory from the will of God. The modern state is usually a democracy, deriving its authority in theory from the will of the people. The social ethics either must be reapplied to speak to the church as the successor of Israel or to the individual as a disciple of Christ, or, as often happens, it must be put aside as belonging to the theory of the theocratic state. Absorbing the ethic of the Old Testament in these three ways, the church can have no pretensions to rule the state. Its task

is the indirect but nonetheless essential one of being the conscience of a state otherwise governed by the principles of
representative democracy.

The nature of the Old Testament as the literary deposit
of a national covenant forces it to make a large place for the
law. It is true that the law is preceded by the saving act of
God and accepted in grateful response to the divine mercy,
so that the Old Testament does know of the grace of God,
and cannot be set over against the New in the sharp contrast
of law vs. gospel. What the New Testament does is to break
the pattern of the Old Testament revelation in which the
grace of God issues in the giving of the law, and replaces it
by one in which the event of Christ issues in the guidance of
the Spirit and the rule of love.

In preaching from the Old Testament, the minister will
often find himself being led by the text to a légalistic conclusion. At this point his gospel compels him to break off the
argument, to dissociate himself from the legalism, and to
point with emphasis to the transformation that Christ has
made in the religion of the Old Testament.

II

Language and Symbolism

Anyone interested in ideas must automatically be interested in language, the vehicle by which ideas are communicated. Certain hypersophisticated minds have developed the prejudice that unless an idea is expressed in the forms and with the logic derived from the Greek philosophers it can have no intellectual status. Drama and poetry may be tolerated, but only as diversions from the serious business of thinking. Such persons are usually rather rude about what they find in the Old Testament, labeling its stories as "naïve" or "primitive" and its prophecy as "disjointed" and "unsystematic."

Granted the premise that logical forms alone are suitable for communicating serious thought, the judgment against the Old Testament is well founded. It contains no formal logic and is poverty-stricken in even the most rudimentary attempts at abstract expression. The classical Hebrew language, and the mind that produced it, worked almost exclusively with nouns and verbs, that is, with pictures of things and descriptions of actions. The Bible writers have a camera's eye, but this does not mean that they have a camera's brain.

Their thoughts are as profound as ours. Only their way of expressing them is not the same as our own.

They use the data of the senses — the sounds, sights, and smells of the world — to carry their message. They cannot take refuge in that bane of all technical writing, the vague abstraction and the convenient label. We might speak of "premature self-congratulation in the absence of the requisite physical and mental capabilities to effectualize it in the concrete exigencies of vital experience." Hebrew is innocent of this welter of adjectives and abstractions and prefers to say, "Let not him that girds on his armor boast himself as he that puts it off" (I Kings 20:11).

The concrete, pictorial quality of his basic documents is both a lesson and a challenge to the preacher. The written word, always before the reader so that he can go back and refresh his memory of the argument that has gone before, will permit the use of abstract terms and technical jargon. The spoken word, delivered in less than half an hour and heard only once, must be crystal-clear at the first hearing, and engaging enough to induce the hearer to go on listening. The technical or philosophical essay can do neither, for if the auditor misses one link in the closely wrought chain of logic he is soon nodding to a lullaby of polysyllables the meaning of which is lost. A picture vividly drawn remains with the hearer because it captures his imagination and he literally "sees" the point.

In working over his sermon, the preacher should remove all the adverbs and three quarters of the adjectives, and translate every abstract paragraph into a picture drawn from life before venturing into the pulpit with it. The increased vigor of the preaching is only one of the rewards. A few attempts at such revision will produce a wholesome respect for the literary artistry of the Biblical authors who write this way as a matter of course.

The challenge of the Biblical language is its antique flavor and unfamiliar ring. The preacher is under an obligation to understand the unfamiliar language and to determine the symbolic value of the imagery. He must decide what interpretation the symbolism may rightly bear, and be on guard against letting an undisciplined imagination carry him beyond the intention of the writers. Then, having understood the message of the ancient writer, he must recast it in terms immediately understandable to the modern hearers. The sections that follow attempt to give some guidance in this difficult task.

BIBLICAL SYMBOLISM

In a linguistic system where pictures convey ideas, the structure of thought must depend heavily on symbolism. Precision and accurate definition give way to connotation and suggestion. Biblical literalism is, therefore, not only theologically indefensible but linguistically incredible. Even the stodgiest literalist realizes that the psalmist's "Happy is the man who has his quiver full of them!" (Ps. 127:5) has nothing to do with archery but is a highly effective image for the protection afforded an aged father by his numerous sons. The symbolic quality of the language is patent here, but in other passages it is less plain, and the literal mind can lose the sense by confusing the imagery with a pedantic statement of fact.

The graphic description of the Lord's descent on Mt. Sinai (Ex. 19:16, 18-19, JE) is full of auditory and visual images.

On the morning of the third day there were thunders and lightnings, and a thick cloud upon the mountain, and a very loud trumpet blast, so that all the people who were in the camp trembled. . . . And Mount Sinai was wrapped in smoke, because the

Lord descended upon it in fire; . . . and the whole mountain quaked greatly. And as the sound of the trumpet grew louder and louder, Moses spoke, and God answered him in thunder.

The conclusion often drawn from this description that Sinai was a volcanic mountain may be true, but it is irrelevant. The trumpet, thunder, fire, smoke, and earthquake are symbols of the divine presence, and if the day of the Sinai revelation had been calm and cloudless the writers would probably still have reported it in the same terms. Any belief later generations may have had in the actual occurrence of these phenomena remains incidental to the faith that the narrative expresses, a faith that does not center in a volcanic mountain under the pall of a thunderstorm, but in the revelation of God to his people. Each in its own way, the physical accompaniments of the Sinai revelation are symbols of what the presence of God meant to Israel.

The sound of the *shōphār,* the ram's horn trumpet, was the call to assembly. When its booming note sounded through the hills, the tribes came together to plan for war or to join in worship. Here at Sinai, God's own trumpet called the nation, not only together, but into existence, in an assembly unique in her history.

The refiner's fire, which burns away the dross and leaves the pure silver, is a common Biblical symbol for God's presence in purification and judgment. In a civilization whose artificial illumination is the lamp, fire is also a ready symbol for the protection, guidance, and revelation associated with light.

Throughout the Old Testament the thunder is the voice of God speaking from his heavenly throne. Its presence in the Sinai narrative shows that the God who now comes to Israel comes prepared to declare his will to them.

The smoke and the cloud are normal accompaniments of the glory of God, which in another passage is said to be present at Sinai (Ex. 24:16-18). The root meaning of "glory" in the Old Testament is "weight," ordinary poundage. It has the derived, metaphoric meaning of "influence," the weight a person exercises in his community. Hence it can refer also to what gives a person "weight," e.g., beauty, wealth, or military prowess. When referred to God, it means the divine weight, the authoritative presence of the sovereign Lord. Wherever the glory of the Lord appears, God is present with the full authority of his royal and creative Presence. The symbols of this Presence are those things which appear to be both heavy and yet detached from and free of the earth, that is, cloud and smoke. Perhaps the best English equivalent of "the glory of the Lord" is "the authority of God."

The piling up of these physical symbols at Sinai tends to frighten the preacher away from the narrative. They are too remote from ordinary experience to be factually convincing. In reality the very multiplicity and awesomeness of the symbols should attract attention to the story, for they are a clear indication that at least the writer thought he was saying something important.

The Sinai experience of Israel is the outstanding Old Testament description of the meaning of the Presence of God. The symbols of the encounter, translated into less spectacular language, mean that at this historic time and place God was present with the full weight of his divine authority to assemble and constitute his people a nation by guidance, by judgment, and by enlightenment. The story is not history in our sense of the word, but theological commentary on history in symbolic form, and its intention can be understood only in those terms.

An unbroken diet of sermons without Biblical basis has trained many churchgoers to confuse a feeling of tranquillity with the Presence of God. Enjoying a pleasant sensation in the viscera while watching a sunset may lead to the rapt conclusion that God is very near. By contrast the Presence of God in the Bible is always the revelation of an authority beyond human authority, and the impelling conviction that that authority is directed to the one who stands before God. It comes with the force of thunder and the judgment of fire, breaks down all pretensions to independence, and brings the one who feels it to his knees.

The "voice of a little silence" heard by Elijah at Horeb after the sound and fury of the elements had died away cannot be used to refute this understanding of the Presence of God (I Kings 19:9-13). Elijah was *expecting* God to appear in the violence of nature. A voice from the lightning and avalanche would have added nothing to the prophet's experience of God, but God maintained with Elijah the sovereign independence of his action. In the lonely aftermath of the storm and into the prophet's forsakenness God spoke, but his word was still the searching, penetrating one of judgment and demand, "What are you doing here, Elijah?" (v. 13).

Biblical symbolism is the attempt of the writers to use the sights and sounds of their daily experience to express a reality that lay beyond the ordinary and gave their experience its meaning. The only way open to their insights is through an honest but imaginative interpretation of their symbolism. The literalistic mind can never find an entry into the sacramental universe in which the Biblical writers lived.

A SACRAMENTAL UNIVERSE

If a sacrament is defined, with John Calvin, as "a visible sign of an invisible reality," the Old Testament presents a sacramental universe. Even the lowliest object in nature can be a signpost, pointing beyond itself to the reality of God.

Soon after his call to prophesy, Jeremiah, still troubled by the implications of his vocation, walked in the orchards of the early springtime. The bare branches of the trees suggested to him the dead, sterile condition of his nation, and the apparent failure of the word of God to bring it to life. This pessimistic reverie was broken by the sight of an almond branch, the first of the trees to come into bloom, covered with the buds of returning life (Jer.1:11-12). The name of the tree, *shāqēdh,* reminded him of a word of similar sound, *shōqēdh,* "watching," and the message became clear to his mind. In spite of the apparent death of all fruitful and productive life, God was watching to bring his will to pass, the one vigilant Power in apparently universal death.

Later in Jeremiah's ministry, the sight of a potter breaking down a vessel that had refused to take proper shape on the wheel became for Jeremiah a parable of God's dealing with Israel (Jer. 18:1-11). If she would not allow herself to be molded to the potter's design, he would smash her to a shapeless lump and remake her nearer to his heart's desire. The prophecy may serve as a warning to the church that it has no inevitable claim on the protection of God. If the church resists God's shaping hand, it too may have to be smashed before it can be made to conform to his purpose.

Jesus' ability to see the ways of God in the seed, the sower, and the yeast was part of his intellectual inheritance, and is to be understood in the same way as Jeremiah's lessons from the world around him.

Neither for Jeremiah nor for Jesus, however, was nature an automatic revealer of God. They were not pantheists for whom nature is God and accordingly speaks its own word about God; nor were they of the sentimentalist school which believes that all one has to do is to look upward to the starry skies to be confronted with deity, ignoring the fact that many will see only little points of light. Religiously speaking, nature can tell a person only what he already knows.

Jeremiah makes this point absolutely clear. God told him to look at the almond branch and the potter's shop, and, having instructed him, also interpreted for him what he had seen. Apart from the fact that he looked at these things with the eyes of faith, he would have seen nothing. Nature speaks of God only as God himself opens the eyes of the beholder to see what is written there. It adds nothing vital to his faith. It rather gives faith a body and a form and a way of expressing itself. Nature, then, is sacramental of God only in a secondary sense, and must rank far behind the traditional sacraments of the church. Nature does not speak of God; but God, the Creator of the natural order, may choose to speak through it. Otherwise it remains the neutral environment in which man's lot is cast.

This understanding of nature could deliver the pulpit and the church from much idiotic waste of effort. The invitations to atheists to seek God among the woodland streams would perhaps be less frequently heard. The practice of filling the minds of children with interesting facts about birds and flowers and calling it Christian education would be less commonly followed. And the special virtue of worshiping God by a lakeside would be re-examined. None of these things is particularly bad until it becomes the cover for the assumption that the saving grace of God in Jesus Christ is too difficult and "theological" for modern consumption and that the same effect can be had by a gentle immersion in nature without the embarrassment of theology.

The Old Testament writers were surrounded by nature worshipers. They never succumbed to the temptation to follow their neighbors in this form of worship because of their allegiance to the principle, enunciated in Chapter I, that the true starting point of religious thought is God, and the primary revelation by which all others are judged and understood is his mighty acts in history. For the Israelite, these were seen best in the deliverance from Egypt. For the Christian, they are made manifest in the appearing of Jesus Christ. In all use of nature imagery and symbol, whether based on the Bible or introduced by way of illustration, the preacher will be saved from deviating from his basic tradition by adherence to the same principle.

A sustained poetic expression of the sacramental view of nature is given by Ps. 104, a poem that comes as close as is possible for the Old Testament to a pure nature hymn. In other psalms, such as Ps. 107, the nature sections are mere preludes or amplifications of the more significant activity of God on the historical scene, but in Ps. 104 nature seems to fill the whole canvas. This may be due in part to the dependence of this psalm on the famous hymn to the Aton of the heretic Pharaoh Amenhotep IV (Ikhnaton). But to see it as merely a nature poem is to ignore the framework in which it is set. It begins with the call to praise, and defines its starting point in unmistakable terms:

> O Lord my God, thou art very great!
> (V. 1.)

In this setting of the majesty of God, learned primarily by his covenant with Israel, the psalmist puts his lively description of the creation of the world and the providence of God extending to all his creatures. In the end, he comes round again to his starting point:

> O Lord, how manifold are thy works!
> In wisdom thou hast made them all.
>
> (V. 24.)

He cannot now stop there. The sense of awe shifts to the spirit of prayer:

> May the glory of the Lord endure for ever.
>
> (V. 31.)

This in turn passes into praise of that distinctive Hebrew kind in which the element of personal commitment and involvement is strong:

> I will sing to the Lord as long as I live;
> I will sing praise to God as long as I have
> being.
>
> (V. 33.)

By modern standards of knowledge the science of the psalmist leaves something to be desired (as ours will to our grandchildren); but within his limited view of nature he has been moved to wonder, and to joyful *recognition* of the handiwork of a God worthy to be praised. It is a judgment on our lack of faith that within our drastically widened scientific view there is often little room for wonder, joy, or praise. "The fault . . ." to quote Shakespeare, "is not in our stars, but in ourselves."

ANTHROPOMORPHISMS

The Old Testament speaks of God in frankly human terms, providing him with all the physical organs and emotional reactions of a very vigorous man. This habit of anthropomorphism is a consequence of the pictorial nature of Hebrew thought. It was not possible for the Hebrew to describe God in terms of pure idea, or to weave a complex of abstractions about him. Even for God there must be a physical counterpart and symbol. This necessity still leaves open the question of what symbol will be chosen, and the Old Testament makes use of a wide variety of images to illumine now one, now another, aspect of God's character and activity. Some of these are drawn from the nonhuman and the subhuman, as when God is spoken of as a rock, a fortress, or a grove of trees. But in the end the only comprehensive image of God is the human being.

Theologically stated, the use of anthropomorphisms follows from the conviction that "God created man in his own image" (Gen. 1:27), the only creature formed after the pattern of the divine. Man, and man alone, is capable of representing God, because he only has been *made* capable of doing so.

Although for both linguistic and theological reasons the Old Testament consistently represents God in human terms, it never commits the error of believing that the reality of God is contained in, or exhausted by, the human metaphor. His immeasurable greatness defies the powers of human speech, so that even the best metaphor is a pale shadow of the reality toward which it points. Isaiah and Hosea, to choose only two illustrations, are unmistakably firm on this point.

> The Egyptians are men, and not God;
>   and their horses are flesh, and not spirit.
>
>   (Isa. 31:3.)

> For I am God and not man,
>   the Holy One in your midst.
>
>   (Hos. 11:9.)

Beyond such explicit denials of the identity of human and divine nature, the reluctance of the Old Testament writers to say what God is like in himself gives a further warning against equating God and man. Recurrent Biblical formulas, apparently descriptive of the nature of God, turn out on closer analysis to be statements of how God acts, the mysteries of his being remaining untouched. God's graciousness, long-suffering, kindness, and readiness to forgive (compare Jonah 4:2) are not so much attributes of the divine nature as qualities of God's action. They are seen, not by philosophical analysis of God's being, but by contemplation of what he has done in and for men upon the plane of history.

The significance of this for the preacher, although absolutely clear, is often ignored. The proper subject matter of a sermon is the deeds of God and what they mean for human existence, with the central focus continually held upon the crucial act of God in Jesus Christ.

Biblical anthropomorphisms, rightly understood, give invaluable guidance to the preacher in his task of presenting God to the people. They are numerous and varied, but each of them has its own special insight into how God acts toward his people.

The image of the *shepherd* (e.g., in Ps. 23) concentrates attention on God's unfailing guidance over a difficult and uncertain road and offers the assurance of care and protection more than sufficient to meet the hazards of the journey. It also makes clear that the leadership of the shepherd must be met by wholehearted trust and complete confidence on the part of the flock that follows him.

In the often-neglected metaphor of the *physician* (e.g., in Ps. 103:3; Deut. 32:39; Jer. 3:22), the Old Testament, centuries before the advent of modern psychology, recognized sin as a disease, the most deadly of human infections. It is a malady, curable not by the couch but by the confessional, and responsive to no treatment except the forgiving love of the Great Physician.

The royal figure of the *king,* expressive of the majesty, authority, and power of God, involves at the same time the all-pervasive paradox of the Biblical faith. The majesty of this king is his moral perfection, his authority is the authority of love, and his power is exercised in acts of deliverance and redemption. The Christian preacher cannot afford to miss the paradoxical nature of the king metaphor, for it is only because of the paradox that he is able to preach " Christ, the King."

The anthropomorphism that represents God as *judge* is falsely considered by many to be characteristic of the Old Testament conception of God. By isolating it from its companion metaphors and by gratuitously inserting the words " stern " or "implacable," they distort the Old Testament religion into a loveless parody of the law court in which an unmoved and immovable judge ferrets out and punishes the minutest offenses according to the strict letter of the law. That there is no correspondence between this caricature and the faith of the Old Testament should be clear even to the most casual reader who has encountered passages such as the splendid declaration of hope in Lam. 3:22-23:

> The steadfast love of the Lord never ceases,
>   his mercies never come to an end;
> they are new every morning;
>   great is thy faithfulness.

Positively stated, the metaphor of the judge expresses the conviction that righteousness and faithful obedience count for something in the world. The universe is not a moral chaos, where any kind of conduct is indiscriminately acceptable. It exists under the governance of a God who examines, weighs, and judges the motives and actions of mankind with an impartiality unswayed by the wealth, prestige, power, or position of the one under examination. The judgeship of God is the Biblical assurance that while man may look on the outward appearance God looks at the heart, and that there is no partiality in his judgment. The New Testament for all its insistence on the love of God makes no attempt to dispense with the metaphor of the judge. Indeed, the most striking use of it is made in the teaching of Jesus (Matt. 25:31-46).

The most inclusive Biblical anthropomorphism is the image of the *father*. Here the authority of the king, the decisiveness and moral concern of the judge, the guidance and care of the shepherd, and the healing of the physician are brought into the context of the family and written together under the single rubric of love. But precisely because this metaphor seems so perfect and complete, the minister must all the more vigorously remind himself and his congregation that it is partial and poor by comparison with the full depth and intensity of divine love.

RELATIONAL NATURE OF OLD TESTAMENT THOUGHT

The God-man relationship is so fundamental to Old Testament thought that almost none of its vocabulary can be understood apart from this relationship. Many words that we define in secular terms, or consider as independent entities, are Biblically unintelligible unless viewed as descriptive of some aspect of the divine-human relationship. Security is normally related to the soundness of the dollar or the size of the insurance policy; peace is a condition of tranquillity on the international scene; freedom is a gift of the state and relates primarily to political liberties; and joy is the same thing as mirth or pleasure.

Biblically, " security," " peace," " liberty," and " joy " are closely related words, each expressing a quality of the human life which has been brought into a saving relationship with God. The nature and implications of this relationship form the whole substance of Christian theology, and it is out of them that the meaning of the Christian vocabulary is derived. The congregation desire and need to know the distinctive meaning of the words that have become central to their faith; and they are rightly impatient when they are given instead homilies on political liberty and international affairs, which they could have had better and more profitably by staying home and reading the Sunday paper. It is therefore a principle of preaching method always to refer religious vocabulary to the content of the God-man relationship, where alone its true freshness and vitality can be appreciated. The following diagram, useful if viewed with a combination of freedom and caution, illustrates the place within this relationship of some of the most weighty theological words of the Old Testament.

In keeping with the conclusion reached earlier in this chapter the circle representing God contains no list of his attributes, but the downward arrow carries the vocabulary associated with his action toward men. The response of the human being, evoked by God's deeds, is described by the words associated with the upward arrow. Human life, transformed by the encounter with God, has the quality described by the words within the circle headed MAN, and the condition of existence when the relationship is broken or non-existent is represented by the words printed outside the circle. None of the groupings is exhaustive. Each can profitably be supplemented by many other terms of similar in-

The Relationship Between God and Man
in the Old Testament

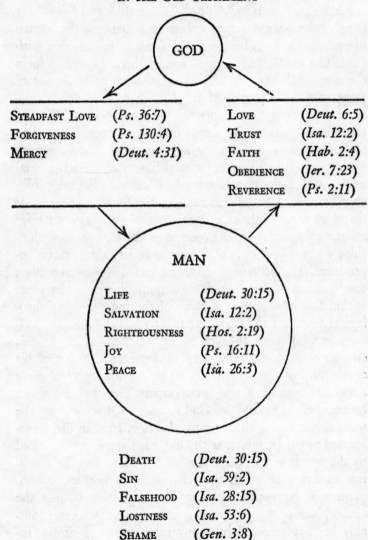

GOD

STEADFAST LOVE	(*Ps. 36:7*)	LOVE	(*Deut. 6:5*)
FORGIVENESS	(*Ps. 130:4*)	TRUST	(*Isa. 12:2*)
MERCY	(*Deut. 4:31*)	FAITH	(*Hab. 2:4*)
		OBEDIENCE	(*Jer. 7:23*)
		REVERENCE	(*Ps. 2:11*)

MAN

LIFE	(*Deut. 30:15*)
SALVATION	(*Isa. 12:2*)
RIGHTEOUSNESS	(*Hos. 2:19*)
JOY	(*Ps. 16:11*)
PEACE	(*Isa. 26:3*)

DEATH	(*Deut. 30:15*)
SIN	(*Isa. 59:2*)
FALSEHOOD	(*Isa. 28:15*)
LOSTNESS	(*Isa. 53:6*)
SHAME	(*Gen. 3:8*)

tent. The Biblical reference in parenthesis beside each word indicates one passage in which its place in the divine-human relationship is vividly expressed. These are intended to be typical, and may be added to, almost indefinitely.

The preacher will readily recognize the homiletical fruit-fulness of the principle represented in the diagram. It indicates, for example, that however much others may treat peace and security as political and economic problems, they remain for the minister basically problems of human existence. When Jeremiah denounced as false prophets those who cry, " Peace, peace, when there is no peace " (Jer. 6:14), he was proclaiming that by breaking its covenant bond with God the nation had forfeited the only possibility of peace open to it, and no juggling of international forces by treaty or alliance could make up for this loss.

In the context of the God-man relationship, salvation cannot be seen as a permanent state arrived at once for all and valid for all time. It exists only within the relationship and only so long as the relationship is maintained. It is no more permanent than liberty, with which it is closely kin. Both disappear together if the saving relationship with God is broken.

The diagram shows righteousness and sin, life and death, as standing in stark contrast to each other. The opposition is, however, more radical than that usually attributed to these words. Righteousness is literally being right with God, and sin is that malicious human rebellion which holds man and God apart from each other. In this contrast, rather than in questions of obedience or disobedience to specific laws, the full Biblical meaning of sin and righteousness resides. Similarly, life and death have little to do with physical survival. Outside the relationship with God, the man most organically alive is a dead man; and within it the frailest of mortals enjoys life. Here is the proper setting for the proclamation of the Johannine promise, " I came that they may have life, and have it abundantly " (John 10:10). Indeed, " the life everlasting " is best preached as a totally new kind of existence beginning when the saving relationship is established, and not as a reward for moral rectitude deferred until after death.

The fear of the Lord is part of man's response to the gracious forgiving and loving acts of God. Such an understanding should serve to dispel the cloud of suspicion that has gathered around the expression. All connotations of cowardice or dread are absent from the fear of the Lord. In their place is awe before the majesty and perfection of God, wonder that his gracious activity should be directed toward persons who are so unworthy of it, and a spontaneous desire to worship and honor him; in short, everything that is encompassed in the best use of the word " reverence." The Old Testament has no word for " religion." The nearest synonym is " the fear of the Lord."

Attempts at precise definitions of the words appearing in the diagram should be avoided. They are flexible and fluid, their meanings easily shading into one another. Life, salvation, righteousness, and peace are virtually equivalent in meaning. Distinctions of emphasis and connotation, rather than of substance, distinguish faith from trust and love from reverence. Sin, shame, lostness, and death are different vantage points for viewing essentially the same condition. Further, the circles and arrows of the diagram are not mutually exclusive. Righteousness may be a quality of God's action as well as of man's response, and within the circle of man every element of the new life is regarded, not primarily as a human quality, but as a gift of God. In addition, trust, obedience, faith, love, reverence, associated with the arrow of human response, are consistently presented as divine gifts. Within the saving relationship and outside the domain of sin and death everything is given and controlled from the side of God, and there is nothing in it that can rightly be said to have any other source.

In the foregoing treatment of the God-man relationship the astute reader will have found lacking any reference to ethics, or any call to the strenuous moral life, and may be wondering whether vigorous ethical drive has been sacrificed in favor of a pietistic and mystical faith. In such a mood it is well to remember that the exhortation to " Rise up, O men of God " is the conclusion, not the premise, of Biblical faith. The diagram contains enough moral dynamic to keep a man out of mischief and busy with the work of God for as long as his life will last. The principle involved is simple but far-reaching. As God has acted toward him, so a man should act toward his neighbor. Steadfast love, forgiveness, and mercy are the hallmarks of the conduct he presents to the world. He becomes a mirror reflecting what God has done for him. The consciousness of being brought into a new life by the grace of God, the commission to represent that new life in word and deed, and the desire to share it with the neighbor is a far more potent ethical motivation than either the fear of hell or the hope of heaven.

Two-Way Words

The traffic on Jacob's ladder went two ways, from heaven to earth and in a return flow from earth to heaven. An important element of Old Testament vocabulary, especially in the area of worship, has a similar double direction. God blesses man, but man may also bless God. God gives glory to his people, and they in return glorify his name. God exalts the nation, and it magnifies him. Men praise God, who is said to *be* their praise (Deut. 10:21).

To speak of blessing God, who needs nothing that man can give, or of magnifying the Almighty, seems both incongruous and presumptuous. But this impression can be sustained only if the words mean the same thing in the two opposite directions of movement. The Old Testament leaves no doubt that God requires no blessing from his worshipers, and that nothing they do or say adds anything to his majesty. It also insists that God is the one source of all blessing and greatness for mankind. The two-way words derive their real significance from these complementary convictions. When the movement is from God to man, they refer to an active revelation of God through his deeds. When the movement is from man to God, the words are passive and receptive, constituting an *acknowledgment* of what God does.

The equivalence of "the glory of God" to the English word "authority" has been indicated above. When God reveals his glory he declares his authority over the universe and mankind. When man glorifies God he acknowledges that God's authority is absolutely binding upon him. In an exactly analogous way God is magnified by a recognition of his majesty that goes beyond empty formulas of fulsome praise to commitment to this revealed majesty. If God is truly almighty, human will and effort must bow to accept his rule. In the act of joyful acceptance God is magnified and exalted.

By far the most frequent of these two-way Old Testament words is "bless." When God is the source and man the recipient, blessing means the outpouring of the divine goodness to meet human need. When man blesses God he acknowledges with gratitude and joy that every good thing in his life is a gift of God. Nowhere is this more convincingly illustrated than in Ps. 103. The psalmist begins with one of the most familiar calls to blessing in the Old Testament:

> Bless the Lord, O my soul;
> and all that is within me, bless his holy name!

He then continues with a recitation of the mighty acts of God that have been directed toward him, all of which speak of loving-kindness, mercy, and redemption. The language of the psalmist makes it clear throughout the poem that the real ground of his blessing is God's own best gift, himself.

The word " praise " does not appear to belong to the same category as do the others, but when it is recognized that praise (*tĕhillāh*) means basically " the vital power of life " it is seen that to praise God is to acclaim him as the source of the vigor, richness, and power of life itself.

In every case, when the direction is from man to God the two-way words belong to the category of response and contain the dual elements of acknowledgment and commitment. There is no end to the possibilities opened up to the preacher by this insight. The authority and blessing of God may be spelled out, and the implications of acknowledging them and committing oneself to them may be pressed home in an almost infinite variety of ways. But beyond this the nature of the sermon itself receives illumination. It is an act in which the preacher proclaims the authority, majesty, and goodness of God in such a way as to evoke acknowledgment and commitment.

III

Out of Slavery

Within the space of fifty years, modern archaeology has opened up the ancient past. The sand-covered mounds of the Tigris-Euphrates Valley, where the thriving cities of Assyria and Babylonia once stood, have yielded hundreds of thousands of clay tablets inscribed with the strange-looking wedge-shaped indentations called cuneiform writing. On these oblongs of baked clay, generations of long-dead scribes had set down business records, contracts, inventory lists, and letters, little thinking that four thousand years later bespectacled scholars of the space age would regard their scribblings as priceless treasure.

Not all the texts come from the world of business. Officials of the temples committed their rituals and mythology to writing so that the sacred actions and words would be accurately preserved. These texts reveal how men of the second millennium B.C. reacted to the perpetual problems of the world, society, and human nature.

THE IMPORTANCE OF BEGINNINGS

The key to a comprehension of the way ancient man understood his world is to be found in the importance he attached to the beginnings of things. A collection of tribal myths, such as Verrier Elwin's *Tribal Myths of Orissa* (Oxford University Press, 1954), is composed almost entirely of stories showing how all the elements in tribal life, from fire to palm liquor, came into existence. The ancient Near Eastern texts have the same consuming interest in beginnings, but in a more sophisticated form, and the name of the first book of the Bible (Genesis, the Book of Beginnings) indicates that the Old Testament writers shared the same way of thinking.

This interest in beginnings is not that of a historian poring " over many a quaint and curious volume of forgotten lore," but of a practical man trying to understand his world so he will be able to live better in it. Knowledge is power, and to know the beginning of anything is to understand its inner essence and distinctive genius, and therefore to have some hope of controlling it to one's own benefit.

Thus, the beginning is not to be confined to any single date on the calendar. The origin of an institution stamped it with a nature and meaning that lasted as long as the institution survived. This almost mystical sense of the timeless quality of the origin of a thing was expressed by projecting the beginning beyond human time and space into the realm of the gods. In this spirit a Sumerian text from the second millennium B.C. reads:

> After the . . . of kingship had been lowered
> from heaven,
> After the exalted tiara and the throne of king-
> ship had been lowered from heaven.

What men treasured or feared most on earth had its origin in heaven, and from the timeless realm of the gods, continuously exerted its influence on the time- and space-bound society of men.

How could this influence coming from beyond the human scene be controlled to the advantage of the earthly community? Ancient Near Eastern thought found the answer in the great temple festivals. In solemn ceremonial the festival re-created the story of the formative event. By thus dramatizing the beginning, it drew the power of the original event down into the presently existing community.

The Exodus and the Cross

Our Bible is heir to this ancient concept of a formative beginning. Both the Old and the New Testament have their distinctive formative event, which imparts its significance and power to every other. In the Old Testament it is the exodus from Egypt; in the New, it is the event of Christ, and especially his sacrificial death and triumphant resurrection. The exodus and the event of Christ are genuine analogues, and from the Christian point of view they stand in a promise-fulfillment relationship to each other, that which was implied and suggested in the exodus coming to its full reality and meaning in Christ. The nature of the analogy may be seen in the common qualities which the two events share.

Both are events in human history. In this respect they stand in sharp contrast to the formative events in ancient Near Eastern mythology. The God of the Bible is no remote deity struggling with other divine powers in the land of the gods, but a *deus agōnistēs,* wrestling in the arena of history with the intractable and rebellious wills of men. God found Israel in slavery in the Egypt of Rameses II, and brought her through "the great and terrible wilderness" to her homeland. Jesus Christ was born in the empire of Caesar Augustus in the days of Herod the king. God acts where men are, in the confusion and struggle of historical events.

In the Biblical perspective, therefore, the events of history are revelatory not only of the deeds and goals of the human race but of the activity of God as well. The Bible is exceedingly reluctant to speak of the inner nature of God. It prefers to draw a veil over the mystery of what God is like in himself, and to tell its readers what God does.

The preacher may be guided by his Bible at this point. Metaphysical sermons, designed to expose the mystery of the divine nature, may impress the congregation with the minister's erudition, but they will always fall short of the gospel. Preaching is not an inquisitive poking and prying into the character of God, but a proclamation of what God has done with his people Israel, and for mankind in Jesus Christ.

The message of a God who makes himself known in events is vital to people who have lost the sense of the significance of day-by-day living. A God of this kind is not to be met in the rarefied atmosphere of abstract thought or in a spiritual life detached from the realities of the world. He will be found where he has always chosen to reveal himself — in the ordinary events of the common day.

Both events issue in the formation of a community. The exodus made Israel; the Christ event produced the church. Israel finds her life and meaning in the law which placed her under the obligation of grateful and joyous obedience; the church, in being the body of which Christ is the head, and the branches of which he is the vine.

In a day when "fellowship" has become a fashionable cliché, meaning little more than "we got together and laughed at one another's jokes," and when the "fellowship hall" is the place where the kitchen is located, it is well to remember that there is no fellowship in the Biblical sense of the word that is not intimately related to the formative event that called the religious community into existence. Glad-handing camaraderie should never be confused with "the fellowship of Christ's sufferings."

Both events constitute a gospel, a saving message which the saved community proclaims. "I am the Lord your God, who brought you out of the land of Egypt, out of the house of bondage" (Ex. 20:2; etc.) occupies a place in Old Testament faith similar to that held in Christianity by Paul's conviction: "God was in Christ reconciling the world to himself" (II Cor. 5:19). The saving act of God in human history, constitutive of the saved community, becomes the redemptive message which that community is charged to preserve and proclaim.

Out of this analysis of the formative beginning an important homiletic principle emerges. The promise-fulfillment relationship between the Testaments is best seen in the analogy between the exodus and the Christ event. It is the Old Testament gospel of the exodus that finds its fulfillment in the work of Christ. Interpreting the significance of the exodus is, therefore, one of the most fruitful ways of illuminating the act of God in Jesus Christ. A study of the exodus gives the Christian preacher the basic themes that he must sound again and again in his proclamation of the New Testament gospel.

THE GOD OF THE EXODUS

The ingredients of the exodus story are simple and commonplace: a slave people spending its strength on the public buildings of the oppressor, a political exile wanted for murder, a daring escape across the desert, and the age-old story of a wilderness people seizing the land of a settled population grown soft from easy living. So a war correspondent traveling with the Israelites might have reported the events. But to Israelite faith there was another ingredient, not visible to the reporter's eye, in their desert adventure. It was a God who saw and cared. The true miracles of the Bible are not God's spectacular appearance in the fire from heaven, but his quiet and unsuspected coming in the simple and ordinary. Nothing is more normal than a baby, and many are born in poverty; God appeared in definitive revelation of himself in just such a babe " wrapped in swaddling cloths and lying in a manger " (Luke 2:12).

As Israel lived out her history under the shadow of the exodus, she came increasingly to see how completely God had described himself in that event.

The God of the exodus is a God of persons. His active concern is for persons rather than for places or things. The deities of the nations surrounding Israel were gods of the storm, of the fertility of the soil, or of the phenomena of nature. They might also be deities of a particular town, country, or region, over which they had exclusive control. The Lord, the God of Israel, was pre-eminently the God of persons, " of Abraham, and of Isaac, and of Jacob." With striking intimacy God calls his servants by name — " Moses, Moses! " (Ex. 3:4); and " Saul, Saul " (Acts 9:4) — as if their individual personalities were of supreme importance to him. The intensity of God's concern for human beings is nowhere more beautifully expressed than in the narrative that prepares the way for the exodus. " I have seen the affliction of my people who are in Egypt, and have heard their cry . . . ; and I have come down to deliver them out of the hand of the Egyptians." (Ex. 3:7-8.)

The God of the exodus is concerned for the helpless.
Ezekiel reminded his people of this fact in unequivocal
terms. He compared Israel in Egypt to a newborn baby,
caked with blood and with the navel string uncut, cast out
in a field to die. In this abject and complete helplessness the
Lord found her and cared for her until she had grown to be
a beautiful woman (Ezek. 16:1-14). Not the merit but the
need calls forth the activity of God. Helpless Israel could lay
no claim upon him, nor had she power or beauty to attract
him to her. It was Israel's very inability to help herself that
moved God to deliver her.

In this unmerited dealing of God with the need of men
is seen the promise of the Christian doctrine of grace that
is so central to the New Testament. The experience of Israel
in Egypt is a concrete illustration of a basic New Testament
truth, " By grace you have been saved through faith; and
this is not your own doing, it is the gift of God " (Eph. 2:8).

In this act of God for Israel one may also see the origin
of the social gospel. The servant of God is concerned for
persons, and especially for the helpless and needy, because
that is the way God acts. His service is called into action by
need, not by merit, because he himself was met and saved
by the loving-kindness of God when he had no virtue or
worthiness to recommend him.

*The God of the exodus is the sovereign Lord of human
history.* He reached into Egypt, and in spite of her ancient
wisdom and the chariots of the Pharaoh, brought out his
people " with a mighty hand and an outstretched arm." The
Old Testament expresses the sovereignty of God in many
ways. He rides the clouds (Ps. 68:4). He scatters the hoar-
frost like ashes (Ps. 147:16). He calls out the stars by number, like a top sergeant mustering his troops (Isa. 40:26).

The most crucial area of his sovereignty is not in nature but in the movement of historical events. He overrules Pharaoh (Ex. 6:1), uses the Assyrian as the rod of his anger (Isa. 10:5), and anoints Cyrus, King of Persia, to do his will (Isa. 44:28).

In the dramatic scene at Belshazzar's feast the writer of The Book of Daniel portrays God's rule in history (Dan., ch. 5). At the banquet table, groaning with rich foods and costly dishes, sit the mighty men of the empire: soldiers, statesmen, and princes. The fate of the world and the destiny of nations seems to rest in the hands of these men. But while they revel, secure in their sense of power, a hand is writing silently on the plaster of the palace wall, "weighed . . . and found wanting." According to the Hebrew faith, that terrible, silent judgment of God always writes the last word in human history.

The preacher who is frightened away from the theme of the sovereign lordship of God in human history by the possibility that it is too abstract and eggheadish for his congregation is abdicating three thousand years of Biblical tradition and selling out to the prophets of humanism and economic determinism.

The God of the exodus is a God who saves. His characteristic activity is deliverance. This is patent on the face of the event itself: God saved Israel from slavery. The centrality of the motif of salvation in the exodus narratives accounts for many elements in them which puzzle the modern mind. The plagues in Egypt (Ex., chs. 7 to 11), the miraculous deliverance at the Sea of Weeds (ch. 14), the giving of the manna and the quails (ch. 16), and the water from the rock (ch. 17) are not mere wonder tales put in to impress the oafs and confuse the intellectuals. They are a heightening and emphasizing of the fundamental message of the narrative: the God of Israel is a God who saves.

With the exodus, the concept of salvation is firmly planted in the Judaeo-Christian tradition, bringing with it the promise fulfilled in Jesus Christ. The recurring sentence, " Let my people go " (chs. 5:1; 7:14, 16; 8:1, 21, 32; 9:1; 10:3-4), contains a whole theology implicit within it. These are the words that the God of the Bible perpetually directs against every aggression or oppression that threatens to enslave or debase human personality, and they are the charter of the Christian's evangelistic, political, and social action.

The God of the exodus is a God of guidance. The triumphant march of the Israelites from Egypt to Canaan was led by a pillar of cloud and a pillar of fire (Ex., ch. 14). In the later days of the exile, the belief that God would one day guide his people back to their land was a powerful source of comfort and hope (Isa. 35:8). New Testament Christians also took heart from this characteristic of God. They felt themselves akin to the Israelites in the wilderness, wayfarers and strangers passing through a foreign land on their way home. This pilgrim faith of the early Christians found a lofty expression in The Letter to the Hebrews. " Here we have no lasting city, but we seek the city which is to come." (Ch. 13:14.) One of our most familiar hymns combines in a striking way the wilderness faith of the Old Testament with the pilgrim faith of the New.

> Guide me, O thou great Jehovah,
> Pilgrim through this barren land.

The God of the exodus is a God who provides. The saving act of God in Egypt and his guidance of the people through the wilderness led to their goal in the Promised Land, which the people were to inherit. Four hundred years after the exodus, Deuteronomy expressed the providence of God in a classic simile:

> Like an eagle that stirs up its nest,
>   that flutters over its young,
> spreading out its wings, catching them,
>   bearing them on its pinions,
> the Lord alone did lead him,
>   and there was no foreign god with him.
>   (Deut. 32:11-12.)

The Deuteronomist gives the lie to all ideas of God's providence as a celestial bread line in which one has only to queue up in order to be fed. The old eagle tears up the nest so that the eaglets cannot remain among the jagged twigs of their former home. The apparent cruelty of this act is designed to force them from security into flight. When the new element proves too much for the young birds and they begin to sink to the ground, the great wings are under them, bearing them up. The providence of God is as much operative in the shattering of false securities as it is in the more obvious form of satisfying human need. The apparently contradictory statements of Jesus: "Take up [your] cross and follow me" (Matt. 16:24) and, "Come to me, all who labor and are heavy-laden, and I will give you rest" (Matt. 11:28), are two sides of the providence of God.

The God of the exodus is purposeful. His activity is directed to the establishment of a community devoted to God and dedicated to carrying out his will. By virtue of her encounter with God, Israel became "a kingdom of priests and a holy nation" (Ex. 19:6). These terms ought to be taken in the reverse order to that in which they appear in the Biblical text.

The holy nation is the nation set apart from all others

because of its special relationship to God and for a special kind of service to God. The words "kingdom of priests" define what this service is. In the ancient Israelite cult the priest was the mediator between God and man. When he came to the altar he brought with him the prayers and confessions of his people. When he turned toward the people it was with the assurance of the blessing and forgiveness of God. It was therefore the duty of the whole nation to stand between other peoples and God, bringing them to God and God to them.

In the Protestant tradition, this element of the exodus faith has been preserved in the doctrine of the priesthood of all believers. More is involved than the banal and essentially egocentric idea that any man can come to God directly, without the mediation of an ordained priest. The doctrine means that every Christian has the responsibility and privilege of bringing his neighbor to God and God to his neighbor. Indeed, the purpose of his own salvation was that he might become the instrument of God in accomplishing this end.

MEMORY

Israel and the church each believed that one particular and definite event in their historic past had shaped them and given them everything that was important in their community life. An event of such momentous consequences could not, however, be regarded as belonging wholly, or even mainly, to the past. It had to be in a real sense the present possession of every generation of the community for all time.

The paradox of an event genuinely belonging to history, but being eternally experienced as a new thing, is expressed in both Testaments by the word "memory." Israel remembers how the Lord brought her out of Egypt (Deut. 8:2), and the Christian takes the bread and wine in remembrance that Christ died for him (I Cor. 11:24-25).

If memory is merely the recalling of factual information, it is obviously an inadequate word to use in connection with such important matters. Some uses of the English word "memory," however, suggest the force it possesses in the Biblical languages. The rallying cry of the Spanish-American War, "Remember the *Maine,*" means more than "Recall as a historic fact that on February 15, 1898, an American battleship was blown up in Havana Harbor." It implies that every American was personally involved in the danger and insult of what happened in Havana Harbor, and that each was called into action to avenge an affront offered to him personally. To remember an event in this sense is to say "It happened to me, and therefore I am committed to the consequences of the event." Thus "memory" means personal involvement and personal commitment.

When the Israelite came to the Temple to present his offering of first fruits, he recited a little summary of the exodus event (Deut. 26:5-11). It begins as a factual account of a past event. "A wandering Aramean was my father; and he went down into Egypt" (v. 5), but as the worshiper feels more intensely his own involvement in the event the pronoun changes from "he" to "us." "The Egyptians treated us harshly, and afflicted us." (V. 6.) When the end of the recitation comes, the identification is so complete that the pronoun becomes "I"; and the worshiper acknowledges that because of what God has done for him, he now makes the grateful offering of his gift. "And behold, now I bring the first of the fruit of the ground, which thou, O Lord, has given me." (V. 10.)

In a closely analogous way the sacrament of the Lord's Supper is a memory of Christ's death. In its ritual the worshiper identifies himself with that event so completely that he can say with Paul, " I have been crucified with Christ " (Gal. 2:20). Having come to the point of personal involvement in Christ's death, the Christian must go on with Paul to the point of commitment. " The life I now live in the flesh I live by faith in the Son of God, who loved me and gave himself for me." (Gal. 2:20.)

THE MEDIATOR OF THE COVENANT

It would be a mistake to represent the saving act of God in the exodus as solely, or even mainly, a transaction between God and the people. The personality and leadership of Moses dominate the Biblical narrative and consistently interpose themselves between God and the nation. The entire weight of the divine presence focuses on this single individual, captures his allegiance, overcomes his timidity, and makes him the human instrument of the great events that are to follow. After the experience of his call, Moses almost reluctantly becomes statesman, orator, general, lawgiver, and theologian, leading, denouncing, and driving the people with superhuman strength.

Some estimate of the importance attached by the Israelite authors to the call of Moses may be seen in the fact that each of the three main writers in the Pentateuch devoted an extended treatment to it. The discussion that follows here is based mainly on the combined narrative of the " Yahwist " and the " Elohist " (Ex., chs. 3; 4). The Priestly version of the event stands somewhat apart in ch. 6:2-9.

Initially Moses had little to recommend him for his high office. He was tainted with the paganism of Egypt, having been brought up in the Pharaoh's court. His hot temper brought his sword too readily from its scabbard, and later caused him to smash the tablets of the law among the rocks at the foot of Sinai (Ex. 32:19). By the laws of any civilized country he was a murderer and a fugitive from justice. Yet the narrative shows that Moses possessed two qualities that made him serviceable to the purpose of God. He had the rare ability to identify himself with his brothers in need. It must have been a shock to the young princeling when he first realized that the Egyptian aristocrats with whom he daily rubbed shoulders in the palace were of a different race than he was, and that his real kinsmen were the slaves who labored on the Pharaoh's buildings. He could easily have turned his back on this unpleasant fact and returned to the good life of the palace. But " one day, when Moses had grown up, he went out to his people and looked on their burdens " (Ex. 2:11). In this moment of maturity for Moses the seed of the exodus was planted.

Moses early displayed the second characteristic that was to mark his work, his consuming passion for justice. It led him to strike down the Egyptian slave master (Ex. 2:12), to place himself between two Hebrews who were expressing their common misery by fighting with each other (Ex. 2:13-14), and to defend a group of shepherd girls against their bullying male counterparts (Ex. 2:16-18), a piece of chivalry that gained him a wife. Moses' conception of justice became one of the pillars of Pentateuchal legal literature — the chief function of law is to protect the weak against the power of the strong.

If Moses is a typical example of the servant of the Lord, it follows that this service does not require the kind of plaster sainthood in which no defect can be found, but rather the willingness to identify oneself with the brother in need and to pay the price of that identification, together with the sensitivity to use power for the aid, not the exploitation, of the weak.

In the context of the exodus the call of Moses has a twofold function. In any revelation of God in history the bare event is ambiguous and requires an interpreter to show that the arm of the Lord is revealed in what might otherwise be seen merely as the operation of political and economic forces. The knowledge of God is not written plain on the face of historical events. It is mediated through human beings raised up in the midst of the events and sensitive to their significance. The call of Moses equips him for the indispensable role of interpreter of the mighty acts of God.

The human instrument of God's revelation is, however, more than a passive spokesman, declaring from the side lines that God is active. He is creatively involved in the events themselves, moving them forward according to God's design. Moses' call is necessarily placed before the exodus begins, for the appearance of this man is a precondition of the exodus. God begins with the man, not the nation, and while his deed is done on behalf of the nation, it is done through the man.

The mediation of the knowledge of God through human individuals is a central idea of Old Testament thought. The priesthood had its Aaron, prophecy its Elijah, the monarchy its David, and the wisdom of Israel its Solomon. The boldness of the prophets in confronting kings and princes was possible because they were convinced that God makes known his will through men of his choosing. Ultimately the Old Testament tradition permits no other form of revelation than that mediated through human personality. The vigorous, temperamental, often violent Moses is thus a promise of the perfect mediation of God's will and power in Jesus Christ. John had this tradition in mind when he wrote, "The law *was given* through Moses; grace and truth *came* through Jesus Christ" (John 1:17).

The call of Moses at Mt. Horeb, standing at the begin-

ning of Israel's formative event, became the prototype for
the divine-human encounter whenever and with whomever
it occurs. The pattern set by this narrative persists with remarkable consistency throughout the Old Testament and
into the New. The experiences of Isaiah in the Temple (Isa.
6:1-9), of Ezekiel by the Chebar (Ezek., ch. 1), of Jeremiah
in Anathoth (Jer. 1:1-10), and of Paul on the road to Da-
mascus (Acts, ch. 26) all consist of the same three essential
elements.

A New Revelation of God. The one on whom God lays
his hand first looks up to see who it is that speaks with him.
With the familiarity of long acquaintance, God calls his
servants by their personal names: " Moses, Moses! " (Ex.
3:4); " Samuel! Samuel! " (I Sam. 3:4); " Abraham, Abraham! " (Gen. 22:11); and " Saul, Saul " (Acts 26:14). The
shock of being so intimately known by one who is himself
unknown creates in the hearer an intense desire to discover
the character of the one who speaks. The experience of being
known by God thus creates the precondition for a revelation
of God in his own terms and on his own initiative.

So personal a revelation could readily become a private
affair, a mystical experience having no relevance to history
and being incapable of communication to others. The Biblical writers are at pains to disabuse their readers of this idea.
The first word that Moses hears binds the revelation to himself inseparably with that to his predecessors and forerunners.
" I am the God of your father, the God of Abraham, the
God of Isaac, and the God of Jacob." (Ex. 3:6.)

" Experiences of God " are so often represented as working the salvation or edification of the isolated individual who
receives them that the Biblical meaning of such experiences
has become distorted. When the God of the Bible speaks,

he breaks down the hearer's isolation and brings him into fellowship with all those who have heard the word of the same God. Each revelation is an incident in the history of God's self-disclosure, a link in a chain forged by God to serve his purpose. The revelation is thus "progressive," moving through history in the hands and minds of faithful men, growing and deepening as it moves, and at the same time joining all who have received it into one community of faith to which the adjective "eternal" is justly applied. In Christian theology this understanding of God's way with his people has been called the communion of saints.

God's first words to Moses express the divine character which is soon to be seen in action in the events of the exodus. "The cry of the people of Israel has come to me, and I have seen the oppression with which the Egyptians oppress them." (Ex. 3:9.) This sentence and those like it in the same narrative (compare ch. 3:7-8) include by implication the nature of God which subsequent events disclose more fully (see earlier in this chapter).

But Moses remains unsatisfied. The awe that made him remove his sandals on that holy ground, mingled with prudential concern for what he will say to the people in Egypt, prompts him to ask, "What is your name?" (Ex. 3:13). As Martin Buber indicates (*Moses* [Torchbook TB 27, Harper & Brothers, New York, 1958], p. 48), the question is more than an inquiry after the proper formula for addressing God. In Hebrew thought the name of a person or thing signifies its nature, and Moses asks in effect, "What are you like?" The answer, "I AM WHO I AM" (Ex. 3:14), is at once a reply to the question and a rebuff to the questioner.

Considerable scholarly discussion has centered in the meaning of the name revealed to Moses. It is often said that the concept of the eternal unchangeableness of God is too

sophisticated for the ancient Hebrew mind. This is undoubt-
edly true of the abstract notion of "eternality," but the related idea of a person whose actions are always reliable and
self-consistent is neither beyond nor absent from Hebrew
thought (see Chapter I). The writer of Ps. 90 expressed it in
a memorable word picture:

> Before the mountains were brought forth,
>   or ever thou hadst formed the earth and the
>   world,
>   from everlasting to everlasting thou art God.
>   (V. 2.)

John of Patmos carried the same thought into the New
Testament. "'I am the Alpha and the Omega'... who is
and who was and who is to come." (Rev. 1:8.)

To know that the God who offers deliverance to Israel is
no fly-by-night deity who may tomorrow change his mind
and cast off the people whom he today adopts, or arbitrarily
substitute hostility for good will, is no small comfort to the
man called to lead the exodus, and no mean insight into
the ways of God. The message remains valid in the age of the
atom and the ballistic missile. Those who stand in the tradition of Moses ought of all men to be least fearful of the extinction of their faith in the blackened aftermath of atomic
war. The final issue of human history is in the hands of the
same God whose unwavering nature is to deliver the helpless, and while we do not know specifically what he will do,
we are confident that it will be consistent with the delivering love revealed in Jesus Christ.

The weight of scholarly opinion leans toward connecting
the meaning of the divine name with the causative form of
the verb "to be," the meaning becoming "I cause to be
what I cause to be." The name thus describes God as one

who comes into history in creative power to create a new thing. Since this is precisely what the Israelites believed the exodus to be — a creative inbreaking of divine power to begin something essentially new — this understanding of the name is a fitting prologue to the exodus. It is, moreover, a promise of the renewed creative appearing of God in the incarnation of Jesus Christ, and of his continued coming into man's personal sorrow and despair to make of him a new creature.

Although the creative coming of God to men and the self-consistency of his action are certainly aspects of the name revealed to Moses, the form in which the name is given preserves the sovereignty and independence of God. The overbold question of Moses is parried, and the mystery of God's inner nature is preserved. He will assuredly act, but in his own way, according to the dictates of his own nature. The little God whose mind can be captured in finite human understanding, whose purpose can be summarized in precise formulas which any schoolboy may memorize, is after Moses an impossibility in the Biblical faith. When human thought and language have done their best he remains shrouded in mystery, and we have seen only the hem of his garment (Isa. 6:1) or the indistinct outline of his presence after he has passed (Ex. 33:23).

A Revelation of Self. The revelation of God brings with it a new self-understanding, and never a flattering one. The collection of false faces, stored in an inner cupboard of the personality to be worn as the occasion demands, is completely stripped away, and the individual stands before God in his naked humanness. His confidence in his own wisdom, goodness, and self-sufficiency is shattered, and he is left with the profoundly disturbing certainty of his complete unworthiness and utter inadequacy. " Who am I that I should go to Pharaoh? " (Ex. 3:11.)

This new self-understanding expresses itself in different ways with different Biblical personalities. Moses fastens on the apparent triviality of his slow and stammering speech (Ex. 4:10). Jeremiah feels little and lonely, a mere lad sent to do a giant's work (Jer. 1:6). Isaiah knows himself as a sinful man involved in the life of a sinful nation (Isa. 6:5). Paul, with his usual blunt honesty, sees himself as a stubborn ass, kicking vainly against the goad (Acts 26:14).

God does not, however, leave his servant in frustration and weakness. Aaron is provided to be Moses' spokesman (Ex. 4:14). The burning coal from the altar cleanses Isaiah's lips, and the hand of God is placed on the mouth of Jeremiah (Isa. 6:6-7; Jer. 1:9). Ananias comes to baptize and instruct Paul (Acts 9:10-19). In each of these experiences the recipient learns that his inadequacy is unimportant, since he is upheld by the sufficiency of God. Quite apart from the specific ways in which God meets the individual need, the final and definitive answer to the human fear and uncertainty is God's assurance " I am with you " (Ex. 3:12; Jer. 1:8). This presence turns the reluctant Moses into the indomitable leader of the exodus, and the hesitant Jeremiah into " an iron pillar, and bronze walls, against the whole land " (Jer. 1:18).

On the Biblical witness, self-confidence in God's presence is the rankest form of self-delusion. It must be cleared away, like the treacherous walls of a decayed building, before the new structure can be raised. Only so will the work that is done be God's work, and not man's, blasphemously taking to itself the authority of God.

A Revelation of Human Need. In the divine-human encounter the eyes never remain turned in on the self. Before the end they are compelled to look out on the world, there to see an area of responsibility and service. This goes beyond a vague humanitarianism diffused over the whole social scene and settling nowhere in particular. It is a definite task in a definite place, as pointed as the word of God to Moses, "I will send you to Pharaoh" (Ex. 3:10); to Jeremiah, "I appointed you a prophet to the nations" (Jer. 1:5); or to Paul, "He is a chosen instrument of mine to carry my name before the Gentiles" (Acts 9:15). In this way the call of God, which, as we have seen, has a prehistory and binds the received into the fellowship of the saints, has also a future and is itself creative of things to come.

To make any one of the three aspects of God's call the whole of religion is to send the faith up one or another of three blind alleys. The *upward look* by itself is a flight to otherworldliness and remains irrelevant to the struggles of humanity on an all-too-earthly scene. The *inward look,* exclusively emphasized, is an egocentric psychologizing of religion, with "mental health" as its ultimate goal. The *outward look,* separated from the other elements, is a social gospel without theological foundation, and, if left to its logical outworking, will reduce the church to an understaffed and ill-trained social service organization, or an association of amateur political analysts. Only when the church preaches the call of God as a *unitary* experience, composed by necessity of these three elements so that self-knowledge and social concern are given in the context of God's self-revelation, can she be herself, and not the handmaiden, or even the prostitute, of some "cause."

IV

Before Abraham Was

Among the most vivid, and sometimes bitter, memories that
survive from Old Testament courses is the recollection of
introductory struggles with the analysis of the Pentateuch.
After a month of wrestling with documentary theories, most
students are ready to curse the memory of Wellhausen, and
to throw in Graff, and possibly Pfeiffer, for good measure.
Many a minister has, hidden somewhere in the recesses of
his library, an underlined copy of the Pentateuch, showing
the documents J, E, D, and P in rainbow hues — a silent
testimony to the zeal of an enthusiastic professor of Old
Testament.

Contrary to popular opinion, such painful studies are not
wasted effort. They mark off the work of certain great individuals or schools of Old Testament writers, and thus
provide the student with a window through which to view
the important strands of Old Testament tradition. Admittedly the analysis may become an end in itself. The colored
underlinings come to life only when they are seen as a
means by which the distinctive ideas of Israel's greatest

thinkers may be isolated and seen in their unity.

In recent years a lively debate has developed around the documentary theory of the composition of the Pentateuch. A group of Swedish scholars, of whom Ifan Engnell is a vigorous spokesman, deny its applicability altogether. But for most scholars the four-document hypothesis remains the basis for discussion, with whatever refinements their ingenuity dictates.

THE YAHWIST

In the prosperous days of Solomon's reign the first Israelite who can properly be called a theologian began to gather the traditions of his people, especially those which centered in the two southern tribes. His sources were myths and legends which careful oral transmission had preserved for centuries. These the Yahwist, or J writer, as this unknown theologian is called, faithfully reproduced, and archaeological discoveries in Palestine have repeatedly illustrated the accuracy with which the flavor and atmosphere of bronze-age Palestine was reflected in these ancient tales. A lesser man than the Yahwist might have ended with nothing more than an anthology of folk stories. But he was more than an antiquarian with his eyes on the past and his back to the future. He arranged his material so as to present it in an entirely new light. By skillfully weaving together the ancient tales, he attempted to show the necessity of God's saving act in delivering the Israelites from Egyptian slavery and in forming them into a nation. His work is a *preparatio evangelium,* a preparation, that is, for the Old Testament gospel of the exodus. The pervasive question of the Yahwist in Gen., chs. 1 to 11, is, Why was God's saving act necessary? or to put it another way, Why Israel?

The Yahwist's answer is one of the most penetrating analyses of the human predicament to come from the pen of any writer. When his work is separated from the Priestly literature in the Pentateuch, it is seen to consist of the following pattern of narratives:

1. The creation of man (Gen. 2:4b-25).
2. The temptation and fall of man (Gen., ch. 3).
3. The first man-slaying (Gen. 4:1-15).
4. God's attempt to deal with evil by destruction — the Flood (Gen. 6:5-8; 7:1-5, 7-10, 12, 16b-17b, 22-23; 8:2b-3a, 6-12, 13b, 20-22).
5. Renewed intrusion of evil — the drunkenness of Noah (Gen. 9:18-27).
6. Pride and confusion — the Tower of Babel (Gen. 11:1-9).

These stories have no obvious historical and chronological connection with one another. Looked at as factual history of the remote past, they are miraculous, mystifying, and singularly uninformative. They begin to make sense when they are regarded, not as external, but as internal history, the natural history of Everyman, showing what happens to and in ourselves.

THE STATE OF MAN

The Yahwist's Creation story often gets bad press because of its portrayal of God in human terms. Folklore is admittedly at work where God is seen molding man from dust and water as the potter makes a clay vessel, breathing into his nostrils to bring him to life, and carving his future bride from a fragment of bone. But the Yahwist is primitive only in his concepts. His analysis of human nature is strikingly contemporary.

Man is a spiritual frog, an amphibian, existing on the borderline between two worlds. On the one hand, he is of the earth earthy, and the clay clings to him and all his works. His very nature makes him a brother to the clod, and rubs his nose in the filth of life. He is not and can never be a purely spiritual or intellectual being. The appetite of the beast and the frailty of the flesh are inescapable parts of his experience. But this is not the whole story of man. He has in his nostrils the breath of God. By the miracle of God's grace he is capable of communication and fellowship with the One who gave him life. The voice of the beast is not the only message which his nature can receive. His inner ear is tuned also to the voice of his Creator.

This two-sided character of human nature means that man can never work or think himself out of his position of dependence on God. He may claim to be the master of his fate and the captain of his soul, but this is self-deception. In the Garden, God provided everything necessary for the well-being of his creatures. But, lest this spate of good things should delude him into forgetting his dependent position, God left man with one firm prohibition. The central tree of the Garden was put outside Adam's control and use. Adam declared his independence, asserted his right to be self-directing, and ate the forbidden fruit.

The Yahwist's vigorous narrative exposes the paradox built into human nature. Helpless in his own strength to fulfill the basic needs of his own existence, he nevertheless has the power to deny his radical dependence on God, and to chart his own course, guided by the compass of his own purposes.

The Yahwist's formulation of the predicament of man is a premise of all later Old Testament writers. It is impossible to preach the prophets convincingly, or even to appreciate what they are saying, unless we can see man as an inveterate rebel against the only valid source from which the fulfillment of his nature can come. The words of Ezekiel, " You consider yourself as wise as a god " (ch. 28:6), and Jeremiah's, " Let not the wise man glory in his wisdom, let not the mighty man glory in his might, let not the rich man glory in his riches; but let him who glories glory in this, that he understands and knows me " (ch. 9:23-24), are only two of hundreds of prophetic statements that have their theological rootage in the Yahwist's analysis of the human state. Isaiah's at first puzzling declaration (ch. 2:12) that

> The Lord of hosts has a day
>> against all that is proud and lofty,
>> against all that is lifted up and high

sees in the lofty merchant ships of Tarshish and the snow-crowned peaks of the Lebanons, symbols of that overweening pride which refuses any implication of dependence and thrusts itself forward into the place of God.

The New Testament sounds the same note as the prophets. " God opposes the proud, and gives grace to the humble." (I Peter 5:5.) The words of the Magnificat (Luke 1:52):

> He has put down the mighty from their thrones,
>> and exalted those of low degree

are more than a cry of triumph from the have-nots of the world. They express the conviction that the mighty, whose might is the sole source of their confidence, have stepped off the road of life and set their feet on the way of destruction.

The Yahwist's understanding of human nature is a rich mine of homiletic possibilities, as varied as the thousand ways in which other Old Testament writers took up and developed the theme. To be alert to its presence opens up the meaning of numerous parts of the Scripture. But it does more. It makes the Christian gospel intelligible. Why the bitter agony of the life of Christ, mounting to its climax of tragedy and horror at Calvary? Something more called the cross into being than man's need for a little help and encouragement as he pulls himself up the ladder of progress. A radical rebelliousness, settled deeply in human nature, called for the most drastic action of God to meet and overcome it. Wherever the cross is thus preached, the figure of the Yahwist stands near at hand.

A comfortable age of climbing living standards and technological progress needs this gospel. Man has shaken free of his immediate dependence on nature, and manufactures his own climate, light, and food. Technical self-sufficiency easily acquires a religious dimension, confronting God with the assertion, " I have no need of thee." But, if the Yahwist is right, the brand of creaturehood is stamped at the center of man's being, and he can no more flee from it than escape from himself. The attempt to deny it leaves the human being lost and alone in a wilderness of his own making, crying out bravely but vainly that he knows the way.

The Course of Temptation

Male egotism has often maligned Mother Eve, blaming the Fall on the fickleness of womankind. To her credit it must be said that Eve put up something of a battle against the serpent, whereas Adam, the prototype of all males, simply took what his wife gave him, and ate. This bit of ammunition for the female side in the eternal battle of the sexes is, of course, not the main point of Gen., ch. 3. The story of the Fall of man presents a searching study of the course of temptation.

The insidious serpent, with his deceitful words and golden promises (ch. 3:1-5), represents the objective nature of all temptation. No one tempts himself. The pressures and allurements of the self-centered life come from outside, and are impressed on the individual by the social structures of which he is a part. The crime-breeding environment of slum, street gang, and blackboard jungle are the serpent's natural habitat. The voice of the rabble rouser inciting to violence, the scurrilous pamphlet playing on prejudice, and the gentle insinuation that one is a little odd if he neglects the fashionable sins are the serpent's doing.

Although the initial impulse to evil is external and objective, the temptation must take root in the individual before it can issue in an outward act of disobedience. How this takes place is graphically shown in Eve's encounter with the serpent. He first convinces her that God's demands are unreasonable. "Did God say, 'You shall not eat of any tree of the garden'?" (Ch. 3:1.) He goes on to assure her that the penalty will not be applied to her. "You will not die." (Ch. 3:4.) Now that the momentum has been established, Eve carries on by herself. The tree is good for food. It is pleasant to look at. It is desirable to make one wise. Already her hand is stretched out, and she has only to pluck the fruit and eat (ch. 3:6).

The psychologists have a name for it — rationalization. The Yahwist would probably have choked on the word, but he knew the reality. There are few people who will say:

> Here's a sin — I'll sin it;
> And here's the price of sinning — and I'll pay.

Most of us are more lily-livered sinners. We have to talk

ourselves into believing, at least for the time being, that it is not really sin, but may even be the mark of virtue. For our own soul's peace we must commit "the final blasphemy":

> To dress the selfish thought, the indolent,
> In the priest's sable and the angel's white.

To be effective, temptation must be taken into the house and domesticated. Therefore, sin is always an affair of the heart. No one saw this more clearly than Jeremiah. He spoke of Israel's sin as engraven on her heart with a point of diamond (ch. 17:1). The corollary to this, as Jeremiah also recognized, is that redemption cannot be realized by tinkering with externals. It too must reach into the inner life. Therefore, Jeremiah's new covenant of forgiveness is also written on the heart (ch. 31:33). The line from the Yahwist to Jeremiah runs on unbroken into the New Testament, and finds unequivocal expression in Jesus' words in the Fourth Gospel: "Unless one is born anew, he cannot see the kingdom of God" (John 3:3).

The rationalization by which sin is brought within the gates of a person's life is never really convincing to the one who makes it. To all others he may appear the best fellow in the world, but he sees himself naked and ashamed. When he is confronted by God he shares Adam's experience. "I was afraid, because I was naked; and I hid myself." (Gen. 3:10.) This concealment from God in the bushes of work, pleasure, or intellectual achievement — a compound of fear, shame, and defiance — is the most disastrous consequence of sin, since it banishes man from life-giving fellowship with God. The New Testament name for it is alienation; and the work of Christ is represented as reconciliation, healing the fear and shame, overcoming the defiance, and bringing man out of hiding into God's presence.

Between banished Adam and Eden, God placed the cherubim and a flaming sword (Gen. 3:24). There is no road back to the innocency man knew before he experienced good and evil. He has tasted the fruit of the tree of knowledge, his eyes are open, and he faces the world with the scars of sin upon him. We mortals cannot know the spontaneous joy of unbroken communion with God. We are knowledgeable, calculating creatures, and our knowledge urges us on to selfish action. The flaming sword blocks our path back to the Garden.

The return to a former golden age when man looked up to God with no doubt in his heart and no question on his lips is not only undesirable but impossible. Paradise is not so simply regained. But, although man cannot be innocent, he can be redeemed. He cannot battle his own way back past the flaming sword, but he can be led into a new and better paradise by the redemptive act of God. In this way the New Testament gospel of salvation rests squarely on the foundation laid for it by the Yahwist insight into the state of man.

CAIN AND ABEL

All the essentials of the Yahwist's view of human nature are present in his stories of the creation and fall of man. What follows merely spells out the fearful implications of the Fall. A generation that has witnessed Hiroshima is likely to agree that the eldest son of mankind was a murderer.

The concise form of the Cain and Abel story in Gen. 4:1-16 leaves out information vital to logical clarity. By what method was the sacrifice made? Why was Abel's sacrifice acceptable, while Cain's was not? How did Cain know that God preferred his brother's offering? The Yahwist was obviously not concerned to give precise data about the form of the cult, or to answer all the factual and theological questions which his story raised. With a minimum of distracting detail he told the story of two men who knelt side by side in the act of worship.

Abel is a shadowy figure. He does not speak or reveal his character in any way. Silent, totally absorbed in the act of worship, he directs his eyes toward God alone. No such fixity of purpose can be seen in Cain. His line of vision is horizontal. He looks at his brother. As he looks he envies; as he envies he hates; and when he hates he kills.

Thus the first murder is the direct consequence of the Fall. When fellowship with God is broken, as it was in Eden, and eyes turn away from God, these horizontal, man-with-man comparisons become inevitable. Man views himself no longer as in the presence of God, but as belonging to a fiercely competitive world of human beings. His standard of comparison becomes the possessions and status of his neighbor, and, when he feels himself unrecognized or inferior, his envy rises to anger and violence. There is Cain in Everyman, from the worshiper who sees only the sinners in the pews, to the dictator who murders a civilization for a place in the sun.

The Yahwist was not alone among Old Testament writers in recognizing that envy produces the soil in which violence and crime flourish. After listing such obvious sins as murder, theft, and fornication, for which the culprit can be caught and put in jail, the Ten Commandments prohibit an unpunishable inner state — covetousness (Ex. 20:13-17). An inspector of detectives could not prove that a man envied the beauty of his neighbor's wife, nor could a citizen be haled into court for wishing he owned his neighbor's cow, but the spirit of covetousness is the first step into the cesspool of violence, crime, and war. With his ruthless shepherd's directness, Amos paints a terrifying picture of the corruption of a nation in which greed had been elevated to the status of policy, where those in power sell " the needy for a pair of shoes " (ch. 2:6), and where noblewomen have only one piece of advice for their husbands, " Give, give " (ch. 4:1). His acid condemnation of Israel returns again and again to the same point. Envy has grown to greed, greed to oppression, and the end of the process is national death (ch. 5:18-20).

The New Testament proposes to deal seriously with this root of violence by restoring that direction of vision which makes it impossible. The man in Christ cannot covet, because he does not have to battle for status in a loveless world or satisfy his ego by outdoing his neighbor. His prize is " the upward call of God in Christ Jesus " (Phil. 3:14); and although life remains a race, he now runs it " looking to Jesus the pioneer and perfecter " of his faith (Heb. 12:2). Life in Christ takes away from the pressures of competitive society the power to start a man on the fatal descent from envy through hatred to violence and oppression. Out of his own Christian experience Paul expressed with precision the new situation that Christ had created for him. " Just as we have been approved by God to be entrusted with the gospel, so we speak, not to please men, but to please God who tests our hearts. For we never used either words of flattery, as you know, or a cloak for greed." (I Thess. 2:4-5.)

THE FLOOD

In 1873, George Smith of the British Museum made a phenomenal discovery among the ruins of ancient Nineveh. He uncovered in the libraries of Asshurbanipal, the last great ruler of the Assyrian Empire, a parallel version of the Flood story. This royal bibliophile had attempted to make a collection of all the literature known in his day, and his libraries contained thirty thousand clay tablets ranging in content from mathematical documents to historical records.

Already in 1857 the combined researches of many scholars had broken the cuneiform script, and the library of Asshur-banipal soon gave up its secrets. Among the most interesting of these was the epic poem, thirteen tablets long, which told the adventures of a god-man, Gilgamesh, in his search for endless life. Journeying westward from the Tigris-Euphrates Valley, the hero came to a land called the Far Distance, where he found Utnapishtim, the only mortal who had been given the gift of deathlessness.

Under the prodding of Gilgamesh's questions, Utnapish-tim revealed how he and his family had been saved from a great flood that had destroyed the rest of mankind. He was warned of the coming disaster by the god Ea, with whom he had found favor, and was advised to build a ship in which to ride out the flood. When he had taken on board " the seed of all living things " and had sealed up the ship, a storm from the south inundated the whole earth, submerged the mountains, and terrified the gods themselves. At the end of seven days the storm passed and the ship ran aground on a mountain. Utnapishtim tested the drying up of the water by sending out birds, and when one of them did not return, he disembarked to offer sacrifice to the gods.

When this text was first published, conservative scholars quailed while more liberal students took heart. Here was a flood story closely parallel to the Biblical account, but much older. (Later discoveries have traced the flood tradition back to a period before 2000 B.C.) As far as the main body of the story goes, the Old Testament version is neither independent nor original. It has drawn on external sources that were the common property of the ancient Near East. The Biblical account is free from the gross polytheism of its Babylonian counterpart, but monotheism is not the most important element of originality in the Old Testament narrative. In order to fit the borrowed flood story into his own distinctive theological perspective the Yahwist provided it with an introduction and a conclusion, in which he interpreted the story in relation to the fall of man.

The preacher is thus well served by the discovery of the ancient Near Eastern flood stories. They indicate for him where his Biblical material is derived and dependent, and where its originality lies. Although interested in pagan parallels to the Biblical story, the Christian interpreter of Scripture will be chiefly concerned with the places where the distinctive Biblical teaching is found, that is, at the beginning and end of the Flood narrative.

The Yahwist's prelude to the Flood story (Gen. 6:5-8) is a brief and pointed statement that after the Fall, the human race had settled firmly into the practice of following its own will rather than the will of God. In Eden mankind had learned " to know good and evil," and the moral decisions made on the basis of that knowledge had uniformly and almost universally fallen out on the side of evil. " The Lord saw that the wickedness of man was great in the earth, and that every imagination of the thoughts of his heart was only evil continually." (Ch. 6:5.) This condition is more serious than the occasional appearance of crimes and acts of violence. The Hebrew word translated " imagination " has overtones of deliberate planning, and the Yahwist's damning sentence may be paraphrased, " The designs and schemes made by men in the private deliberations of their own inner lives always and everywhere ran counter to the intention of

God." The Yahwist thus made the implications of the Fall universal. As Adam in his disobedience is Everyman, so Everyman in his heart is Adam.

The Yahwist's description of Noah's contemporaries contains the doctrine of the total depravity of man in a rudimentary form. The idea is not that human nature is so rotten as to be incapable of isolated acts of goodness and kindness, but that all thinking, feeling, willing, and doing carried on in isolation from God is tainted with self-interest and warped by self-centeredness. The doggerel lines, often taken as an expression of man's essential goodness, are in reality a statement of man's depravity:

> There's so much good in the worst of us,
> And so much bad in the best of us,
> That it hardly behooves any of us,
> To talk about the rest of us.

It is not the good in the worst of us, but the bad in the best of us, that constitutes the moral problem, and makes true Paul's words, "All have sinned and fall short of the glory of God" (Rom. 3:23). The doctrine of total depravity means that there is no one who can go along under the power of his own inherent righteousness without the continuous support and forgiveness of God.

In the Babylonian flood story the deluge comes because of the caprice of the gods. The only explanation offered for its origin is that "their hearts led the great gods to produce the flood" (tablet XI, line 14); and in the sequel, Enlil is accused by the divine assembly because "he, unreasoning, brought on the deluge" (tablet XI, line 168).

For the Yahwist, the destruction of mankind resulted from the moral nature of the God of Israel and from the seriousness with which he viewed human sin. The increasing wickedness of mankind posed a problem for God. His

daring experiment in making creatures capable of fellowship with himself had failed. He had produced instead a
race of rebels. The obvious corrective would be to make a
clean break and a fresh start by the total destruction of
mankind. With grief in his heart, the Lord changed his
mind (KJV, " repented"; RSV, " was sorry") about his
human creation, and took the decision to wipe it out of
existence by flood (Gen. 6:6-8).

In the Yahwist's perspective, the most important fact
about human existence is that in the movement of historical
events the human actors are morally responsible before the
sovereign Lord of history. The ultimately destructive forces
which raise the storm of confusion and disorder and bring
man's carefully constructed houses tumbling about his ears
do not arise from economics or politics, but from rebellion
against God.

But God's action in history is not the blind use of uncontrolled and irresponsible power. The Yahwist holds that the
Lord of history is self-consistent, not capricious. He reacts
as vigorously to preserve righteousness as he does to bring
judgment against evil. Hence Noah's righteousness puts
God on the other horn of the dilemma. To destroy the good
with the bad would be as morally inconsistent as to let sin
flourish unchecked. Noah must, therefore, be spared.

The moral consistency of God to which the Yahwist's
flood narrative gives vivid pictorial expression is a fundamental tenet of Old Testament and Christian theology, in
both of which it takes its place as the one sure foundation
of hope. " God is faithful" (I Cor. 1:9; compare Deut. 7:9;
etc.) is the guarantee that man is not grinding out his years
in a world insensitive to his moral struggle. The moral
stance of an individual human being has cosmic significance,
and goodness possesses genuine survival value, because God
himself conserves and cherishes it.

The faithfulness of God is the presupposition also of the Biblical doctrine of immortality. God will not throw away, because of the incident of death, the creatures over whom he has labored and in whom the seeds of obedience have begun to take root, albeit among many weeds. The Lenten message of the church also rests on the faithfulness of God. He will not permit the perfect righteousness of the Christ to be washed under by a flood of hatred, nor allow Pilate and the mob shouting " Crucify him " to have the last word. The third day comes.

The conclusion of the Biblical flood story (Gen. 8:20-22) formally resembles that of its Babylonian prototype. In both, the survivor of the deluge builds an altar and offers sacrifice. The scene would provide a powerful subject for a modern artist. The world built by man's self-centeredness has collapsed and fallen. No clear or meaningful line can be seen in the picture, in which all form has been reduced to chaos. The jagged remains of shattered buildings, temples, towers, and towns, are jumbled together in twisted shapes of ruin.

Yet if this scene was put on canvas, it would only partially represent the Biblical view of reality. The artist would have to place in the center of the picture, drawn with full realism, an altar with a family bowed in worship — apart from the altar, formlessness and chaos; at the altar, meaning and direction. In this worshiping family the scattered elements of the broken world will be gathered into a harmony and unity. The scene constitutes a parable of the ways of God with men.

THE DRUNKENNESS OF NOAH

After his escape from the flood, Noah settles down to grow grapes, and becomes overfond of his own product. In a drunken stupor he exposes his naked body to the gaze of his sons. Shem and Japheth refuse to look at their father's shame. Ham shows no such reserve, and for his disrespect *his son,* Canaan, is doomed to be the perpetual slave of his uncles (Gen. 9:20-27).

This unedifying little tale comes from a strand of tradition hostile to the agricultural way of life of which the vine is the symbol; it gives a justification for the depressed status of Canaanite elements in the later Israelite nation; and it reflects the Hebrews' horror of nakedness. The story gives the white race no divine mandate to keep the Negro in subjection. To use it in this way is to provide yet another illustration of justifying human brutality and stupidity by proof texts from the Scriptures.

None of these motifs fully account for the Yahwist's interest in the story. Crude as it was, it filled a necessary place in his thought as the postdeluvian equivalent of the Fall. The Flood had not wiped out human sin and left the pure stock of the righteous Noah to people the earth with saints. The tendency to rebellion had been an undetected stowaway on the ark, and with the novel temptation of the vine it had made a victim of Noah himself. The experiment of destruction, having failed to purify mankind, was never to be repeated (Gen. 8:21). God must seek another way to subdue the continuing rebellious spirit of man.

THE TOWER OF BABEL

Before moving on to the beginning of redemptive history in God's dealings with Abraham and his family, the Yahwist pauses to sum up his understanding of the human predicament. The story of the Tower of Babel, a typical Yahwistic mixture of naïveté and profundity, leaves the reader in no doubt that the human problem is basically that of self-centered, self-confident pride in man's capacities and achievements.

Working with the meanest of building materials, bitumen and baked clay (they do not possess building stone), the men of Babel are nevertheless sure that they can make a permanently enduring city and a tower whose top will reach heaven (Gen. 11:3-4). In this venture, their aims, though heady, are superficially valuable and attractive. They wish to guarantee their present unity and to establish for themselves a lasting reputation. With their bricks and mortar they will build their way to heaven, and set themselves in God's place, famous and united.

The Yahwist is often charged with childishness because he represents God as ignorant of what goes on on earth. His apparent simplicity may, however, be simply his way of emphasizing the complete isolation from, and indifference to, God's purpose to be found at Babel. The project is so independent of God that he is even ignorant of its purpose.

The literatures of the world throw off Utopias as a grindstone throws off sparks. Everyone seems to have his own patent medicine to cure the world's ills, and his own private ladder to heaven. The reign of justice and peace, we are assured, waits only for a wise and cultured use of human resources in the establishment of a unified and permanent civilization.

With this point of view the Christian preacher, the heir of the Yahwist, cannot agree. All utopian schemes for human self-betterment are towers of Babel. Their end result is the exact opposite of what was intended. Instead of producing unity, the builders broke apart into warring groups, unable any longer to understand one another (ch. 11:7). Instead of establishing their permanent fame, they left as a monument an unfinished tower, its ruined top staring at the heaven it could not reach. Man reaches heaven only because God brings him there, not because he builds his own ladder.

Implied in the scattering and confusion of Babel is the hope that God will one day restore order and unity to his disordered creation. Luke saw in the infant church the fulfillment of that hope, and recorded his conviction in the story of Pentecost (Acts 2:1-8). The workers laying bricks for the Tower of Babel hear their fellow laborers break into unintelligible speech. Equally mysteriously, those who heard the preaching of Peter each received the message in his own language. Pentecost is Babel in reverse. The community of those in whom the spirit of God has replaced the spirit of pride, and who serve Christ rather than the goals of fame and progress, is the agency by which God will heal the confusion and disorder of mankind.

The Yahwist's primeval history provides the Christian preacher with the negative side of his message — the state of man apart from God. These incisive analyses of the nature of man, of the way temptation takes root in him and issues in violence, of the faithfulness of God in dealing with both good and evil, and of the disordering power of pride are foundational not only to Judaism but to Christianity as well. With the passage from Gen., ch. 11 to Gen., ch. 12, the Yahwist turns from the negative to the positive. The alienation of man is met by the call of Abraham and the beginning of Israel's redemptive history.

V

The Forerunners of the Covenant

THE NATURE OF THE DOCUMENTS

In the patriarchal stories of Genesis (chs. 12 to 50), as in the prehistorical material, the specter of Wellhausen and his documentary analysis raises its head and must be dealt with. But once more the suspected enemy turns out to be an ally, and an understanding of the literary structure exposes new preaching potential in the stories.

The literary situation in Gen., chs. 12 to 50, is more complex than in the earlier chapters of Genesis. The sections dealing with Abraham (chs. 12 to 25) are rather loosely structured, being composed of a succession of separate stories hooked together by connective sentences but not really unified. With the account of the life of Jacob (chs. 26 to 37), the narrative tightens up and becomes more coherent and continuous until, with the Joseph stories (chs. 38 to 50) it becomes a fast-paced, flowing narrative that reads like a novelette.

The complex interweaving of traditions that produced

this literary structure requires some word of explanation. In Gen., chs. 12 to 50, the work of the Yahwist again provides the theological and literary groundwork of the narrative. All its essential elements are from his pen. However, his good example in preparing a collection of early traditions of Israel had been followed by a like-minded author (or perhaps school of authors) in the Northern Kingdom. By about 850 B.C. the northern part of the nation was in possession of an account of the tradition and folklore of Israel parallel to the Yahwist's work in the south, and called in scholarly shorthand the E (for Elohist) document. Somewhile after, probably about 650 B.C., a redactor or editor brought the two documents J and E together into a more or less continuous narrative.

The redactor was more than a scissors and paste compiler, who sat in a study clipping parts out of the two books before him and fastening them together with the ancient Israelite equivalent of Scotch tape. In his own way he was a creative artist, doing his work with insight and skill. He selected those parts of E which filled up the gaps in J and arranged the different elements of his material so as to interpret its meaning to the reader. Out of the work of the redactor, which might easily have been wooden and mechanical, come two of the most imaginative and vigorous portraits to be found in the literature of any nation, that of Abraham, the hero of faith, and of Jacob, the rogue who became a saint. The insights involved in the redactor's work are the subject matter of the present chapter. The Priestly material added later to the JE document is not considered.

In order to appreciate the genius of the redactor of JE it is necessary to look briefly at the special problem posed for Israelite historians by the patriarchal tradition. On the basis of strict logic the Old Testament should begin with the story of the exodus and the work of Moses. These events formed the nation and laid the basis of its social, legal, and theological structure. But in historical matters pure logic has a way of being submerged beneath the necessities of the facts. Recent researches into the early history of Israel have made it virtually certain that not all the groups which later made up the nation were descended from the people who had fled from Egypt. Many elements of the Israelite population filtered gradually into the territory of Palestine from the desert fringes after about 1400 B.C., and were already in the land with a tribal organization and with long-established traditions and places of worship when the fugitives from Egypt arrived about 1225 B.C. Historic Israel thus consisted of two major elements: those whose traditions went back to Moses and the exodus, and those who initially did not share in this tradition, but whose national lore centered in Palestine itself. The patriarchal tradition, revolving as it does around sacred places on the soil of Palestine, most likely originally belonged to the group whose ancestors had never been in Egypt.

Early in her history Israel faced the problem of fusing these separate strands of her heritage into a unity. Long before the work of the Yahwist, the basis of a solution to this problem had been worked out. The patriarchal tradition, centered in Palestine, was made preparatory to the exodus tradition; and the covenant of God with Abraham, Isaac, and Jacob was represented as an anticipation and a promise of the national covenant between God and Israel in the time of Moses. The Yahwist, followed by the Elohist and the redactor, adopted this way of organizing the tradition, so that in our Bible the magnificent compilation of the patriarchal stories stands as a prelude to the national covenant.

By this process the Hebrew historians introduced into the Judaeo-Christian heritage the concept of "a covenant of promise." Initially the motivation may have been a desire for national unity in a population of varied origin and tradition. In the end, the work of the Old Testament writers furnished the New Testament church with the means for understanding its relationship to the nation Israel. In the first chapter of this book the relationship between the Old and New Testaments was stated in terms of hope and fulfillment. This hermeneutical principle is not imposed upon the Scriptures from the outside, but is stated explicitly in the Biblical documents themselves. For the Hebrew writers the patriarchal tradition stood in the same relationship to the Mosaic covenant as for the Christians the Old Testament bears to the New: hope to realization, preparation to finality, promise to fulfillment.

THE CALL OF ABRAHAM

As he reflected on the history of his people from his new vantage point within the Christian faith Paul was captured by the figure of Abraham in whom he saw a genuine Old Testament anticipation of Christianity. The apostle's obsession with Moses as a legalist prevented him from seeing clearly the emphasis on salvation by the grace of God which underlies the exodus narrative. But in Abraham, Paul found exactly what he was seeking, a man who was declared righteous on the ground of faith alone, before the law existed. Accordingly in his exposition of the Old Testament, Paul represented the covenant of promise as prior to and more basic than the covenant of law, and Abraham, rather than Moses, as the authentic type of the Christian.

The call of Abraham at Haran in the extreme north of

the Fertile Crescent (Gen. 12:1-4a, J), repeated in Palestine (ch. 15, an intricate combination of J and E), reveals the implications of a covenant of promise.

Both versions of the call of Abraham are built around the promise of the multiplication of his descendants into a great nation (chs. 12:2; 15:5, 18). Many preachers are repelled by the gross nationalism implied in the promise, and the apparent favoritism shown by God to this one man and his family. Neither of these impressions touches the full meaning of the passage.

The promise that existed between God and Abraham was to be fulfilled in the remote future and in a distant land. The God who could make and fulfill such a promise must be independent of space and time, and in control of the time process. He could not pledge the future unless the times were in his hand (Ps. 31:15). The psalmist's metaphor is a telling one. God holds time in his hand as a person might hold a book. He is uncontrolled by it and able to manipulate it to his own purpose.

A commentary on this aspect of God's character is given later in the story of Abraham when God reveals himself to the patriarch at Beer-sheba under the name " El Olam " (Gen. 21:33). The usual translation of the name, " the Everlasting God " (KJV and RSV), does less than justice to the meaning of the title. " Everlasting " suggests duration in time, mere unendingness. " The God of eternity," a more accurate translation, indicates ownership. Time and space are God's possessions and set no limits upon his action. He is sovereign Lord of time. It serves his will and responds to his command.

The prophets, and especially the Second Isaiah, repeatedly reminded their hearers that the God of Israel is the ruler of time (Amos 5:8; Hab. 2:3; etc.). They did so with reason, for God's control of the temporal process was the charter and guarantee of the genuineness of prophecy. The prophets' often thankless task was to declare the consequences of sin. From the human point of view a consequence is always future. If what lay ahead were shaped by human action alone, no basis existed for the prophetic word. The king and the people might be right and the prophet tragically wrong. However, the validity of prophetic preaching was guaranteed because God, the Lord of time, declares the end from the beginning (Isa. 46:10).

THE CONTENT OF THE PROMISE

1. *A New Thing.* On the human side, faith, born in the encounter with the God of the future, carries the conviction that something new has appeared in history. In the case of Abraham this is obvious to the point of triteness. Although he would never literally see its actualization, Israel came into existence in him. Israel's starting point was his act of faith. Abraham could not look beyond the curtain of the years to Sinai, Calvary, and the long record of the triumphs and disasters of the Christian church; but in a sense more real than the chronological, they began with him.

This conviction of Abraham has a vital message for the contemporary world where people are so often oppressed by the meaninglessness of life. Whenever God touches a person, in that moment something new and significant begins. A train of events is set in motion by the act of faith, of which the end result can neither be seen nor predicted, but which has permanent meaning in the purpose of God. Because of this peculiar quality of the act of faith the author of Hebrews can say " Faith is the assurance of things hoped for " (Heb. 11:1). Thus, Biblically, faith and hope are inseparable. Faith opens up the long view and reveals the far horizon, because it lifts the isolated, mortal human being out of his hopelessness and meaninglessness and makes him part of the ongoing purpose of the God of eternity.

2. *The Promise of Blessing.* The call of Abraham contains the promise, "I will bless you, and make your name great" (Gen. 12:2, J). The eye is caught too easily by the benefits that Abraham will receive through his faith. A world-renowned offspring will write his name large across the pages of history. The passage is less interested in the blessing than in the source of the blessing. Three times in one short sentence it hammers home the point "I [God] will do this."

The redactor of the Abraham story leaves his readers in no doubt that the blessing was operative in the patriarch's life. He consciously and deliberately portrays Abraham as a man of outstanding dignity and moral excellence, head and shoulders above his contemporaries. His unselfishness in giving the choicest grazing land to his youthful and ambitious nephew, Lot, produces a sentence not unworthy to serve as a motto for the United Nations, "Let there be no strife between you and me. . . . Is not the whole land before you?" (Gen. 13:8-9, J). Toward kings and kinsmen and slaves Abraham behaves with the nobility of a man who knows his life to be directed by the same God who controls the course of history. He is by no means perfect. His weak yielding of Sarah to the Egyptian king (ch. 12:10-20) and his brutality toward Hagar (ch. 16:1-6) were reprehensible even by the moral standards of his own day. Nevertheless he appears as a man of inner strength and nobility, serviceable to God because of his faith.

The worth of a man is what God makes him to be, and his nobility and dignity are his because God makes him so.

The reverse does not hold true; his brutality and weakness are his own doing. This is the frustration and glory of the Christian's life. All his achievements are God's and all his failures are his own.

3. *A Shared Blessing.* The call of Abraham also involves the sentence, "Thou shalt be a blessing" (Gen. 12:2, J); and the grammatical structure of the sentence represents this as the *consequence* of the blessing given to Abraham. The privilege is not given for self-enjoyment or self-aggrandizement, but that through the patriarch the blessing might reach out to others. The idea of a shared blessing was so important to the J writer that he reiterated it in the next verse, "By you all the families of the earth shall be blessed."

It is remarkable how firmly Paul's roots are sunk in the Abrahamic theology. His cry, "Necessity is laid upon me. Woe to me if I do not preach the gospel" (I Cor. 9:16), is a direct reflection of it. The gospel with its unsearchable riches had been given to Paul. He became a compulsive preacher, intensely aware that the blessing was given in order to be given away. Paul is thus the spiritual father of the Christian missionary enterprise. The sharing of the grace of God in Jesus Christ is not an option for the Christian community. It is the very life of the church, for the one who hugs the blessing of God to his own breast soon finds that he is embracing a skeleton from which the flesh is gone and the life has fled.

THE NATURE OF FAITH

Abraham's response to his encounter with God is faith. He heard a command, he was given a promise, and he committed himself completely and unreservedly to the consequences of the command and the promise. He indulged in no bargaining with God, and allowed himself no backward glance. The Biblical text summarizes Abraham's act of faith in words of deceptive simplicity, " So Abraham went, as the Lord had told him" (Gen. 12:4, J). The faith of Abraham transcended mere belief, with which faith is so often confused. To be sure, the response of Abraham implied a profound conviction of the trustworthiness of God, but it went beyond belief to action. In Abraham, faith can be seen in its true nature — adventurous and total commitment to the consequences of an encounter with God.

The preacher has the difficult task of preventing the concept of faith from shriveling up into intellectual assent to dogma or from vaporizing into so-called practical " do-good-ism." One of his best safeguards is recurrence to the basics of faith as seen in the Abraham story: the self-revelation of God (the divine initiative that makes faith a possibility), conviction of the trustworthiness of a God who reveals himself, commitment to the demands and claims of God, and commission to share the blessing and the promise with others. In this understanding of faith the centuries-old controversy over faith and works becomes an irrelevance, since works have no longer an independent status. Works and faith can no more be separated than breathing and life, and works have no meaning in themselves except as they witness to their source in faith.

Abraham's faith was " reckoned to him as righteousness" (Gen. 15:6). This sentence is a fragment of the J source attached by the redactor to what is essentially an E version of the call of Abraham. It illustrates the acute theological insight that informed the redactor's work. Righteousness, here as elsewhere in the Old Testament, refers to the rightness of a man's relationship to God, his stance toward the moral ruler of the universe. Ethical bookkeeping in which the ledger of good and evil deeds shows a balance either in favor of, or against, an individual ceases to be of interest to the writer. He is concerned with the solution of the underlying ethical problem. There is one posture of life which includes within itself the totality of moral and ethical conduct. This is faith. If a man is standing right and walking right before God, the details of his conduct may be left to take care of themselves.

Any sermon that offers a pep talk on helpfulness and kindness is degenerate, because it understands neither righteousness nor faith, nor their relationship to one another. The Christian minister makes his unique contribution when he holds firm to his gospel that righteousness is a quality of life which comes into existence only in the experience of faith. (See p. 52.)

The Test of Faith

The sacrifice of Isaac (Gen. 22:1-19) is one of the few long sections of the E document woven into the Abraham story. The redactor deliberately placed it at the point where interest turns from Abraham as the recipient of the promise to Isaac as the heir of the promise. His reason for inserting the story at this place is made clear in the opening sentence, "God tested Abraham." What happens subsequently is therefore to be understood as a trial of Abraham's faith.

The command to sacrifice his son may have been pressed upon Abraham by the religious environment in which he lived. Human sacrifice was a common feature of Canaanite religion in the second millennium B.C. The patriarch may well have asked himself whether his God demanded less of him than the deities of the cities near which he pitched his camp; or whether, if he withheld the human sacrifices that the pagans offered, his devotion to his God was not inferior to theirs.

By whatever means and under whatever religious and social pressure Abraham arrived at the terrible conclusion that he must kill his son, he accepted it as a command of God. The acceptance forced upon him the cruelest of dilemmas. To obey the command meant to lose the promise. Isaac was his only son, born unexpectedly in his old age, and he could not hope for another heir. Yet the promise involved not only Abraham himself but the generations who would arise after him. When he plunged the knife into the body of Isaac he would cut off that very posterity upon which the blessing depended. On the other hand, to disobey the command would be to forfeit the ground on which the promise had originally been given. Unreserved and instant obedience was the act of faith by which the promise had been received. To hold back before this new command of God would be to prove himself faithless, and to break, perhaps forever, the relationship with God in which the promise had come.

The E writer gives no indication of the struggle that must have raged in the mind of the patriarch before he reached his decision. Abraham remained a man of faith. Hearing, or believing he had heard, a clear command of God, he ignored the consequences to himself and his family and obeyed.

To argue the right or wrong of God's demand on Abraham is to miss the point of the story. The patriarch's ignorance of God's purpose, his misunderstanding of God's true nature, and the cruelty of the act he was called on to perform are necessary literary devices to bring into boldest prominence the triumph of Abraham's all-conquering faith.

In the presence of a hideous misconception of the will of God, against which the combined force of self-interest and paternal love protested, Abraham nevertheless obeyed. Nowhere in the Biblical record is the principle of "God before self" more startlingly illustrated.

After the first word of command, stark and unexplained, God falls silent and Abraham is left alone. The story drops sharply from heaven to earth. The familiar details of common life are meticulously listed: the early rising, the saddling of the animals, the cutting of the wood, the journey, the climb of father and son together to the sacred place on the mountaintop. But over the narrative hangs the ominous shadow of the sacrifice; and it breaks through in the boy's ironic question, "Behold, the fire and the wood; but where is the lamb for a burnt offering?" (v. 7), and in the father's unconsciously prophetic answer, "God will provide himself the lamb for a burnt offering, my son" (v. 8).

When the point of no return is reached and the sacrificial knife is about to fall, the action of the story rises abruptly from earth to heaven; and the voice which has been silent is again heard, "Do not lay your hand on the lad." In this new revelation the fear and doubt of Abraham are removed, and he learns something new about the character of the God whom he has been called to serve. He is not like the gods of the pagan cities who require the blood of children to satisfy their claims to lordship. The God of Abraham desires to bless without destroying.

The episode on Mt. Moriah offers a clue to the process of religious growth. Abraham received a revelation of God partial and distorted, misleading to the point of untruth. Yet he acted upon it, and in his response he received a new and fuller revelation of the character of his God. Had he rejected the first demand, unreasonable and savage though it was, he would have remained convinced that he had to deal with a cruel and arbitrary deity who demanded the life of his son.

The story of the sacrifice of Isaac is an epitome of the history of the people of God. God's self-revelation is met with the response of faith, and in this response a new revelation is made possible. This revelation in its turn elicits a renewal of faith, and still further revelation follows. So from Abraham to Moses, from Moses to Amos, from Amos to Hosea, and from Hosea to Isaiah of Babylon, knowledge of God builds and increases in power and depth until the way is prepared for the coming of Christ.

This is not progress in the ordinary sense of the word, since it is not a growing structure created by human effort. Nor is it strictly progressive revelation in which God gauges accurately what man is capable of receiving and gives him insight according to his capacity. It is more dynamic than either of these. Neither a calculating God nor a resourceful mankind determines the process. It exists and moves forward by and in the personal relationship of faith.

What is observable in history is also determinative for the individual. If a man waits until his knowledge of God is complete and all his questionings are answered, he will never move from the place where he is. It is total commitment to what is understood, perhaps mistakenly, to be the will of God that gives life direction and motive power.

ISAAC

The redactor apparently knew very little about Isaac that was worth telling. He was born, got married, tended his flocks, dug wells, and died. His strong-willed sons, Jacob and Esau, gave him a good deal of trouble, but this is no novel experience for a father. Isaac is a commonplace man, his ordinariness emphasized by his position between the noble Abraham and the flamboyant Jacob.

Quiet and unspectacular though his life was, it provided an indispensable link in the chain of witness from Abraham to Moses. By simply receiving the tradition of the promise from his father, keeping it alive in his family, and passing it on to his son, Isaac did the one thing which no one but he could accomplish. If this ordinary man had failed in his rather mundane responsibility, the hope that began with Abraham would have come to an early end.

The Biblical authors are consistent in their emphasis on the importance of the continuity of witness; and often to the boredom of readers who resent long lists of " begats," they trace meticulously the human line by which faith was transmitted. In the New Testament too the significance of the commonplace man is fully recognized. The author of II Timothy, in what appears to be a conscientious effort to summarize the most pressing duty of the Christian, wrote, " What you have heard from me before many witnesses entrust to faithful men who will be able to teach others also " (ch. 2:2). This is precisely what the Isaacs in the Biblical tradition accomplish. Though no supreme sacrifice and no spectacular heroics are required of them, their quiet testimony, generation by generation, is as essential as the blood of the martyrs to the survival of the church.

Sermon illustrations which hold up to the congregation the examples of the heroes of the faith often fail in their intention. There are few Luthers and many Isaacs in the pews, and Isaac may be left wondering what relevance the example of the great man can have for him. He will probably spend his days under the attrition of a continuous round of petty duties and the pressure of minor temptations, and will never be called on to declare his faith before the whole world in a moment when the destiny of the church is in the balance. He may easily get the impression that there is a hierarchy among Christians with the giants at the summit, the lesser heroes below, and himself far down the line. An order of merit may be applied to scholarship lists or business organizations, but it has no place in Christian thought. In the divine economy what is required of a man is not that he be spectacular or successful, but that he be faithful. Therefore, Isaac stands with Abraham and Jacob on equal terms.

The Pilgrimage of Jacob

The young Jacob was a master in the art of deception. It seems almost as if his first reaction on meeting a stranger was to develop a scheme for getting the better of him. He successfully applied his shrewd, calculating mind to swindling his brother, his father, and his uncle. Only a determined and single-minded shyster would take advantage of his father's old age and blindness callously to deceive him in the last few days of his life.

The tradition regarding the early character of Jacob is a feature of both the J and E document. Esau's sale of his birthright to scheming Jacob is from E (Gen. 25:29-34), but the account of the deception of aged Isaac is the redactor's composite treatment of both his sources (ch. 27). Some commentators excuse Jacob's conduct on the ground that it was not reprehensible according to the popular morality of his own day. The redactor could not, however, have included it in his narrative without feeling the tension between the conduct of Jacob and the command "to honor thy father and thy mother." It must be concluded on both counts that the redactor intended to say exactly what he seems to say. The youthful Jacob was a swindling rogue.

The life story of Jacob must, therefore, be a study in the development of his character, or in more precise language a study in conversion. This conclusion raises the question, Where, in the several chapters devoted to Jacob, should we look for the crucial points in his experience? The fact that Hebrew thought begins with God and proceeds from that starting point to man directs us at once to Jacob's two great encounters with God, the one at Bethel (ch. 28:10-17) and the other at Penuel (ch. 32:22-32). In both cases the present form of the story is a result of the redactor's conflation of J and E, and whatever theological insight the stories contain is due to his genius in shaping them and placing them in their present position in the narrative.

A comparison of the two stories shows at once that the second carries more weight than the first. The revelation at Bethel had little effect on Jacob himself; but when he had wrestled with the man at the ford of the River Jabbok, he was literally not the same person. He left the struggle, no longer Jacob, but Israel. In Biblical thought a change of name is the outward index of a radical change in character or status. The redactor's treatment of the two theophanies is a clear statement that after Bethel, Jacob was essentially unchanged, but that after Penuel his character was radically transformed.

At Bethel, Jacob encountered the God of Abraham and the promise was renewed to him. His experience was a startling one. Jacob believed that he had run beyond the jurisdiction of his grandfather's God; and the last thing he expected was to find that from the place where he slept, fearful and alone, the traffic between earth and heaven, invisible to his waking eyes, nevertheless went forward. He now felt himself to be in the most sacred place on earth, the very gate of heaven, and he was moved to reverence and awe.

But the hardened man of business was still there. The unexpected presence of God might be turned to personal advantage. Jacob's vow is surely one of the most bare-faced attempts on record to squeeze the last drop of profit out of religion. If you will be with me, and protect me, feed me, clothe me, and bring me home in peace, you shall be my God, and — in a burst of generosity — I will give you a tenth. God did not reply.

Bethel led Jacob to the knowledge that he was a man of destiny, the heir of the promise. It assured him that wherever he was, God was close at hand. But Jacob received the revelation passively. It remained on the surface of his consciousness, intellectually accepted as true, but it did not penetrate deeply into his nature and worked no basic change in him.

Jacob's subsequent dealing with Laban showed that his fine, deceptive hand had lost none of its skill. Laban was no senile Isaac and could, if necessary, display some tricks of his own, as Jacob found on his wedding night when the head on the pillow next to him proved to be that of Leah and not her beautiful younger sister, Rachel. But this was only a temporary setback, and in the end Jacob had Laban's two daughters, the best of his livestock, and the title deeds to his property (the household gods).

Jacob now approached his home again, and the old fear of Esau's vengeance was strong upon him. He made arrangements for the safety of his family and flocks and waited the night, alone as he had been at Bethel, beside the Jabbok. In the night he wrestled with a man. At the dawn he left the place, injured and limping, but a different person.

The story is an extremely primitive one, and its literary

history can be reconstructed with a fair degree of probability. In its pre-Israelite form it told of a struggle between a human hero and a night-prowling demon who had to be gone to his home in the stream before the break of day. By holding the deity until sunrise the hero was able to force it to do his bidding. This tale was preserved at the shrine near the Jabbok because it told how the place got its name and why the limping dance and the prohibition of eating the flesh of the thigh were features of worship there. The story was adopted by the Israelites when the wrestler was identified with Jacob and his opponent with the angel of the Lord.

The literary history does not, however, account for the redactor's use of the story or for the central place which he gives to it. Jacob, who had received the first revelation of God passively, now wrestled with the whole force of his being against the God who had blessed him. He was hurt, but he continued to struggle; and in the wrestling, Jacob, the shyster, disappeared, and Israel, the striver with God, emerged. He had tricked the blessing from Isaac, received it passively from God; now he wrestled for it, and it penetrated deep into his nature and became a part of himself.

The experience of the Jabbok transformed Jacob's relationship with his brother Esau. The new man no longer fled from his brother, nor devised some new means of deceiving him. He came forward frankly and openly with conciliatory words and gifts. " Accept, I pray you, my gift that is brought to you, because God has dealt graciously with me, and because I have enough " (Gen. 33:11). If conversion means a turnabout, a reorientation of life, Jacob is a converted man.

It is significant, however, that the conversion is not achieved by a single approach of God to the patriarch. God's second touch is required before the work is complete, and a substantial part of a lifetime lies between the two encounters. The way of God with men is misrepresented by a theology in which conversion is always instantaneous, always irresistible, always complete. The human being clings tenaciously to his self-centeredness, and to break its grip upon him may require that God return to the attack again and again. The complacent Christian, who holds that his conversion is behind him and that the work of God in him is finished, may in fact be standing between Bethel and the Jabbok, intellectually aware of the presence of God but still holding the citadel of his inner being as his own private possession.

Jacob's experience also warns against the expectation that conversion is casual or pleasant. Transformation of a life involves the destruction of things cherished and the tearing out of deep-rooted habits and attitudes. Jacob, limping from the Jabbok, testifies that it comes with pain and struggle, often with personal hurt. The birth of the new man involves the death of the old, and Paul was using no idle metaphor when he said, "We are crucified with Christ." The pulpit has been too much concerned with "selling" Christianity as a quick and painless route to peace and joy. The deception usually takes in no one but the preacher, for those who reflect upon it know that such preaching offers no solution to any problem of human nature, but only a tranquilizer to deaden man's sensitivity to his own plight. The hurt and pain, the bitter wrestling in the night, must be faced before the dawn breaks on a new man.

sponsibility to fellow human beings, it will lack the power and depth of a morality which arises from the conviction that life itself is a trust from God and that its every action is to be weighted and judged with reference to him. The concluding lines of John Milton's sonnet on his twenty-third birthday reflect the same spirit as Joseph's rejoinder to Potiphar's wife.

> All is, if I have grace to use it so,
> As ever in my great Task-Master's eye.

VI

The Prophetic Movement

The institution of prophecy was well known in the ancient world. When an Egyptian official named Wen-Amun came to Phoenicia about 1060 B.C. to buy cedar wood for the Pharaoh, he was ill-used by the independent king of Byblos, Zakar-baal. Wen-Amun was saved from further indignity by a youth of the court who, seized by prophetic frenzy, announced that the visitor from Egypt was under the protection of the god Amun. In Babylonian temples the *barû* regularly gave prophetic oracles as part of the normal operation of the *cultus,* and the four hundred fifty prophets of Baal who served Jezebel were functionaries of both court and temple (I Kings 16:32; 18:19). The royal entourage of King Ahab contained at least four hundred prophets of the Lord who informed the king what was God's will in all important matters of statecraft and war (ch. 22:5-12).

The principal distinguishing mark of the ancient Near Eastern prophet was that he was the mouthpiece of the god whom he served. He was able, when in a prophetic state, to speak the will of his patron deity. Israelite prophetism shared this quality. The Hebrew prophets were the voice of the Lord, the God of Israel, among men. This interpretation of the prophetic office appears clearly in the call of Jeremiah. "Then the Lord put forth his hand and touched my mouth; and the Lord said to me, 'Behold, I have put my words in your mouth.'" (Jer. 1:9.)

What marked off the great prophets of the Old Testament from the prophetic functionaries of other religions was their loyalty to the distinctive covenant faith of Israel. Their uniqueness is not in their office, which can be duplicated in many other religions, but in their interpretation of the meaning of that office. While the Old Testament provides numerous examples of prophets who were content to be advisers to the priests of the temple or to the king on his throne, the men who make up the backbone of the Old Testament prophetic tradition were consciously spokesmen of the covenant God to the covenant people.

The prophets thus appear basically as preservers of the covenant tradition and not, in the first instance, as innovators. Their insistent and often repeated word to Israel was "Return" (for example, Isa. 21:12; Jer. 4:1, 18:11; Hos. 6:1), by which they meant, "Renew your loyalty to the covenant on which the existence and meaning of Israel rests." This call was issued in the midst of a desperate struggle against the infiltration into the covenant faith of the theology and way of life associated with pagan religions. In the attempt to preserve the faith against the intrusion of foreign elements the prophets enlarged, reinterpreted, and brought new meaning to the ancient covenant faith of their people. In attempting to be preservers they became pioneers.

It is perhaps always true that the real innovator, the genuine pioneer, is not the one who tosses the past aside like a worn-out garment and avidly pursues every new thing.

Such an attitude can easily degenerate into the worship of novelty for its own sake. All that is old is not bad, and all that is new is not ipso facto superior. The real pioneer is the one who, like the prophets, seeks to make the old values and insights speak with an authoritative voice in a new age, and to reshape them, if need be, so that their relevance is felt in a new generation.

THE WORD THAT CAME

The question of the nature of revelation is one of the most acute problems of theological thought, and is central to any understanding of the prophetic movement. It is therefore important for the preacher to consider carefully how the prophets themselves described the revelation which they received. The formula " The word of the Lord came to me saying " occurs so frequently in the prophetic books that it is often ignored as a mere preamble to the message, like the mumbled " Let us pray " of some worship services. The familiar translation does less than justice to the meaning of the prophetic formula of revelation. A more literal translation, while less elegant, conveys better the force of the original Hebrew: " The-word-of Yahweh was toward-me in-order-to-say."

Word and Spirit. " The word " is the characteristic Old Testament designation for the means of inspiration which the prophet felt active upon and within him. It is surprising that the prophets rarely use " the Spirit of the Lord " with this meaning, and then only in the late and dying days of prophecy. It is instructive to see why this is so.

In Hebrew as in Greek the word translated " spirit " also, and basically, means " wind." The Spirit of God is the wind of God. The wind has three connotations or associations that make it a suitable word to describe divine activity. It is invisible. It is powerful. And it is uncontrollable. When the invisible and uncontrollable power of God entered a human being he was said to be under the influence of the wind, or Spirit, of God. The coming of the Spirit bestowed new powers on the one who received it, or heightened his normal powers to a superhuman degree. So the Spirit came to be regarded as the great charismatic, or gift-giving, agent of God.

During the Israelite settlement in Canaan (1200-1020 B.C.) the Spirit of the Lord was regarded as giving fantastic and extraordinary powers to certain chosen men. The wild, ecstatic dances of the primitive prophets, their whirling, raving ecstasies, the torrent of meaningless words that poured from them, were manifestations of the powerful and uncontrollable wind of God which had seized them and was buffeting them about (I Sam. 10:9-12; I Kings 18:25-29). Samson's enormous strength reached superhuman heights and he became a savage engine of destruction when the Spirit visited him (Judg. 14:6, 19; 15:14-15). In all probability the prophets used the Word instead of the Spirit to describe the inspiring power that came to them from God mainly in order to avoid just such bizarre connotations.

When, however, the early meaning of the word "Spirit" was in part forgotten, it returned to use in prophetic literature, still carrying the idea of an invisible divine power that gave gifts to men, but now the quieter and more inward gifts of truth, guidance, and light. Out of this later and less spectacular use of the word "Spirit" the Old Testament contributes to the New Testament understanding of the Spirit of God and of Christ.

A definition of the activity of the Spirit (which is also a

sermon outline) would contain the following elements. The Spirit is the invisible power of God under his sovereign control and not at the disposal of man, by which God is present with men in illumination, guidance, and inner nourishment.

He (the Spirit should not be spoken of as "it") illuminates by inwardly interpreting the purposes of God. Paul and John are at one on this point. The apostle states it in sweeping form:

> "What no eye has seen, nor ear heard,
>   nor the heart of man conceived,
>   what God has prepared for those who love him."
> God has revealed to us through the Spirit. For
> the Spirit searches everything, even the depths of God.
>   (I Cor. 2:9-10.)

The Evangelist records it as a promise of Jesus to his disciples: "When the Spirit of truth comes, he will guide you into all truth; for he will not speak on his own authority, but whatever he hears he will speak, and he will declare to you the things that are to come" (John 16:13).

The Spirit guides by inwardly motivating the person who receives him to live by the purposes of God. Paul states it succinctly: "All who are led by the Spirit of God are sons of God" (Rom. 8:14). He saw the practical day-to-day life of the church as controlled by the Spirit. "To each [member of the church] is given the manifestation of the Spirit for the common good." (I Cor. 12:7.)

The Spirit offers that nourishment which is true life, transcending mere existence and developing the vital powers of the personality to the full. "To set the mind on the Spirit is life and peace." (Rom. 8:6.) Such a life is freed from all the lesser allegiances and tensions that might enslave it, so that Paul is able to say, "Where the Spirit of the Lord is, there is freedom" (II Cor. 3:17).

The Imparted Life of God. The Word and the Spirit have similar basic connotations. A spoken word is intimately bound up with the breath of the one who utters it, and ancient man had an almost mystical feeling about the breath. Breath is life. When a person dies his breath ceases, but while he lives it plays about his lips and nostrils like a small wind. Its coming and going is an index of the psychological state of the person. When he is angry or excited it comes fast from his lips, and when he is in repose it moves smoothly and evenly. A word is a bit of the breath, shaped and sent out by the one who utters it. Talking was, therefore, a serious business for the ancient Hebrew, since every word he spoke contained a fragment of his own life.

The life of a person, sent out in his word, was an active agent, carrying with it the power to do what the word said. When an army sergeant shouts "Halt" and the recruits on the other side of the parade grounds stop as one man, we have our psychological explanations of what happened; but to the ancient Hebrew mind it is a simple case of the sergeant's word going out from him, entering into the soldiers and stopping them in their tracks. The power of the Word of God to fulfill itself is reflected in the familiar text from Isaiah:

> [My word] shall not return to me empty,
> but it shall accomplish that which I purpose,
> and prosper in the thing for which I sent it.
> (Ch. 55:11.)

This view of the word as an active power accounts for the Hebrews' dread of lying (see Jer. 27:10). The liar does something worse than misrepresent facts. He identifies his own life with what is false and destructive, and sends a part of himself into the world to do an evil work. Moreover, he declares to all that his false word springs from a corrupt life. This ancient psychology of the word has something of value for our own time in which falsehood has become an accepted instrument of political policy, and lies, a normal part of business and social life.

The Word of God is part of the life of God, gathered up by him and sent out from himself. What the prophet received was, not so much a meaningful message to be repeated to the people, as a fragment of the divine life which had entered into him, so that Jeremiah can compare it to a burning fire in his heart (Jer. 20:9).

The Mystery of the Word. "The-word-of Yahweh *was.*" The verb "came" in English translations of the prophetic formula is an attempt to convey the peculiar meaning of the Hebrew verb "to be." This verb is ordinarily omitted in a Hebrew sentence. When it does appear it usually means "to come into existence." The prophetic formula thus means that the Word of God came into existence in the consciousness of the prophet.

Here the impenetrable mystery of the Word is safeguarded. The prophet cannot explain it as a sound heard by his physical ear or as a sight relayed from eye to brain. He does not know how it comes, but he is sure that a part of the divine life has come into existence in the midst of his mortal and human life. Jeremiah had often been in the street of the potters, but on one such visit the clay on the potter's wheel became inexplicably symbolic of the nation, and a word of God came into existence (Jer. 18:1-11).

Prophetic inspiration is not hearing articulate sounds

which are then repeated mechanically as a phonograph record, so that the human syllables are the actual syllables of God's speech and the human meanings precisely God's meaning. It is the much-more-mysterious coming into reality of the divine life in the mortal life of a completely human being.

Within the framework of Christian preaching the presentation of the Word as the imparted life of God is a valuable corrective to the grossly mechanical views of inspiration which seem to be Biblical but in fact are not. It is also a means of understanding the religious insights and inspiration that may come to any believer. The prophets were not equipped with a supernatural receiving apparatus for hearing the word of God not given to other men. The same word, in its mystery and saving power, may come into existence in the life of any sincere servant of God.

Objectivity and Purposefulness. Anything that exists in the mind can easily be interpreted as merely a product of the mind. The prophets were quick to safeguard the objective reality of what had come to them, and to repudiate the possible accusation that they had produced the Word by their own mental processes. Indeed, according to Jeremiah, it was the "false prophets" who passed off the visions of their own minds as the Word of God (Jer. 14:14; 23:26). The rather large task of insisting on the objectivity of the Word of God is accomplished in the prophetic formula by a single preposition: "The-word-of Yahweh was *toward*-me." The preposition is *el*, most commonly used to express motion toward. Originating outside themselves the Word of God moved toward and into the prophets.

The last element of the formula is what is technically called the infinitive construct with the preposition *le*, a standard Hebrew way of expressing purpose. The Word came "in-order-to-say." Its coming was no accident. It came with purposeful and deliberate intent to accomplish a definite end. The call of Jeremiah strikingly illustrates the purposeful coming of the Word.

> See, I have set you this day over nations and over
>   kingdoms,
> to pluck up and to break down,
> to destroy and to overthrow,
> to build and to plant.
>
> (Ch. 1:10.)

The sense of mission is the inevitable result of the coming of God's Word. The almost monotonous recurrence of the command "Arise and go," following human encounters with God in the Old Testament, makes it clear that receiving the Word of God is not a fuzzy and ill-defined emotional experience, not an amorphous "good feeling" or "religious feeling." God's Word has come to accomplish God's intention, and it makes the recipient the agent of that purpose.

Summary. Protestant theologians from Luther to Barth have centered their theology in the doctrine of the Word of God. One of the most helpful ways in which the preacher can approach this fundamental theme is through the prophetic formula, "The word of the Lord came to me, saying." The Word of God is the life of God himself, imparted to and entering into the lives of men. It is not produced by human reflection but comes objectively to the recipient and lays on him the responsibility of discharging the will of God which the Word reveals. The preaching of the Word of God in this sense can never be without its effect.

Jesus as the Word. Something of the life of God entered the prophet for a brief period only, and with a specific purpose. This partial and transient inspiration is, nevertheless, a promise of the incarnation. In the human figure of Jesus Christ, God projected himself purposefully among men for their salvation. Christ is the *complete* prophet. He not only receives the Word; he is the Word. In him, as the Fourth Evangelist wrote, "The Word became flesh and dwelt among us" (John 1:14).

THE PROPHETIC STRUGGLE

No reader of the Old Testament can fail to be impressed with the sense of urgency that breathes from every paragraph of the prophetic messages. The prophets felt that they were confronting their people with the issues of life and death. For them the choice between the Lord and Baal was not an academic theological problem to be settled in the quiet detachment and sweet reasonableness of a discussion group. Yahweh and Baal, the God of Israel and the idols, represented two incompatible ways of life, between which no adjustment and no compromise was possible. In this crisis of decision Israel could not "go limping with two different opinions" (I Kings 18:21). She must choose whom she would serve.

Modern Baalism draws the same sharp lines as did its ancient counterpart, and the need for the prophetic note of urgency remains. Not an ersatz, pulpit-beating fervor put on for the occasion by a preacher who is otherwise quite satisfied with things as they are, but a frank and incisive statement of the issues involved. No preaching is true to the prophetic tradition if it does not confront the people with the either-or of the prophets.

The Lord or Baal? The city of Ugarit stood in ancient times at the extreme north of the Phoenician coast. Within its walls a bustling, wealthy mercantile civilization flourished from 2000 B.C. to the twelfth century B.C. From its now silent and deserted ruins the industry and skill of a French archaeological expedition, led by Dr. Claude Schaeffer, has recovered the material remains of a once great city. Among the most spectacular of the finds is a series of religious and ritual texts, inscribed on clay tablets. The people who wrote them were Canaanites. Their religion was the same Baalism that has left its mark on almost every prophetic book of the Old Testament. The anvil on which prophetic theology was hammered out was four hundred and fifty years of continuous struggle against this Baalism. Since the discovery of the Ugaritic tablets the nature of the Baalism against which the prophets contended has become much clearer, and by contrast with it the central concerns of the prophetic faith stand out in bold relief.

The Nature of Baalism. To the Canaanite mind religion existed to harmonize human society with the great rhythms of nature on which the well-being, indeed the survival, of the community depended. Since the powers that presided over the natural phenomena were the high gods, the problem resolved itself into getting the deities to work for the benefit of their human subjects. In the agricultural society of Canaan the key figures among the deities were mighty Baal, the Rider of the Clouds, who brought the autumn rains and made the earth flourish and yield her increase, and Mot, the somber Lord of Death, whose power was felt in the dry season when the vegetation withered and the land languished in the grip of death. The regular recurrence of these two seasons — the life-giving rain and the withering heat — was interpreted as a reflection into the natural world of a battle, eternally repeated, between Baal and Mot. When the death god was victorious and Baal lay dead, the earth was barren and lifeless. When Baal's warlike sister, Anath, struck down Mot and Baal returned to life, the fertility of the land was reborn.

This alternate victory and defeat of the productive forces of nature was by no means automatic. It needed to be helped and assured by the religious acts of men. Every year the king and his priests, marshaling all the magnificence that their city could boast, publicly enacted the great drama of Baal's death, resurrection, and triumph. They did this, not in the spirit of theatrical entertainment, but in deadly earnest. If the ritual were not conducted, Baal might not rise and the fertile land would lie forever under the grim rule of death. Through its cult drama, Baalism ensured that the powers of nature would operate for the good of men.

The annual ritual just described is " sympathetic magic " in the grand manner. One of the basic characteristics of primitive thought is devotion to the principle that " like produces like." To obtain a desired result it is only necessary to imitate that result in a ritual act. Thus, vigorous shaking of branches and the pouring out of water on the ground will cause rain to fall, provided the imitation of the storm is accompanied by the proper ritual incantations.

Manifestations of the working of sympathetic magic less splendid and pretentious than the cult drama of Baal and Mot were found everywhere in Canaan. At the " high places " scattered throughout the land the local Baals, whose special care was the fertility of the soil in the immediate neighborhood, had to be charmed, cajoled, and coerced into doing man's will. Unlovely indeed to the eyes of the prophets were the methods used. The altars smoked, the priests and prophets of the shrines declared the will of the deity, the sacred prostitute plied her trade and her patrons congratulated themselves on having stimulated the soil to reproductive power.

The Relevance of Baalism. The relevance of this ancient faith for today lies in the two foundation assumptions on which it rested: (1) religion exists to make the gods serve men and (2) the principal function of religion is to preserve the *status quo*. These are distortions of religion to which the Canaanites can lay no exclusive claim. In them the spirit of Baalism revives century by century, and in the constant challenge to oppose them in the name of the living God the prophetic struggle is forever renewed.

1. *Baalism represents control of God rather than service to God.* It therefore appears whenever the question is asked, " What can I get out of religion? " as if religion existed merely to deck the path of our mortal pilgrimage with primroses. Yet it must be admitted that much that passes for religion, or worse, for Christianity is of this Baalish kind. The temple of Baal stands secure on many religious bookshelves where textbooks of orthodox Baalism turn the religion of the cross into a set of tricks and techniques for harnessing the power of God to the desires of men. Christianity is turned into God's great bargain basement, where for a modest investment of time in church attendance and a modicum of daily prayer and Scripture reading one can buy peace of mind, calm and repose of spirit, and a safe haven from all the perils of life.

The prophetic question is not, " What can I get from God? " but " What does the Lord require of you? " (Deut. 10:12; Micah 6:8). If he should require that we face a cross, we cannot on that account conclude that he has failed us and look to a more amiable deity, not quite so demanding in his claims. This is not to say that there is no harvest of blessing for the servant of the Lord. The fruit of the Spirit makes an impressive list: "love, joy, peace, patience, kindness, goodness, faithfulness, gentleness, self-control" (Gal. 5:22). But the Baalist looking only at the blessing forgets the cost. He confuses cause and result, and serves God in order to obtain these advantages. It follows according to Baalish logic that if the benefits are not forthcoming on schedule, faith has failed and may be abandoned.

Baalism worms its insidious way into prayer. The approach to God then resembles sending an order to a mail-order company. It goes on the proper form, of course, but with the expentancy that it will be filled in detail and that there will be no delay or deficiency in the service. An extension of Baalish prayer is the belief that if a large enough group is assembled and prays hard enough, God's hand will be forced and the requests granted. The theology behind such prayer must conceive of God as a celestial senator, who, if he receives enough letters from his constituents, will be compelled to do something about the lamentable state of the roads.

There is no desire in what has been said to undercut the place of prayer in the Christian life. "The prayer of a righteous man has great power in its effects." (James 5:16.) But the prayer of such a man is, like the Lord's Prayer, prefaced with the words, "Thy will be done," and ends, like Jesus' prayer in Gethsemane, "Not my will, but thine" (Luke 22:42; Matt. 6:10). The central petition is that, if the prayer runs counter to the purpose of God, he will deny it, and in his mercy correct the faulty faith of the one who prays.

2. *Baalism stands for things as they are; prophetic religion for the ongoing purpose of God.* The religion of the Canaan-

ites, geared to the recurrent rhythms of nature, was a cyclic thing. Each year the wheel spins once. As it dies at the end of its motion, religion with its rites and ceremonies gives it the push that sends it round again for another revolution. Like the wheel of fortune at a carnival the Canaanite wheel of history turns on a fixed axis. It starts nowhere. It goes nowhere. Its meaning is exhausted in the fact of its endless repetition. Thus Baalism, ancient and modern, stands under the spell of things as they are, and is dedicated to their perpetuation ad infinitum. It is content if next year is the same as last. Only in bad times is its voice raised in protest, and then it sounds no higher note than a longing for " the good old days."

To the prophetic mind this is religion in reverse, a patchwork of perversion and error. It misunderstands altogether the significance of history. History is not a wheel but a road, an ongoing process ruled by the will of God. It was, however, no part of the prophetic intention to declare that human history expresses perfectly the design of God. This would be to dismiss cyclic Baalism with one hand only to welcome the subtler Baalism of evolutionistic humanism with the other. It is only a step from the contention that history expresses the will of God to the comforting blindness that " every day and in every way we're getting better and better." In Charles Dickens' memorable phrase, to say " everything that is, is right " is virtually to declare that " nothing that ever was, was wrong."

What happens in history is the resultant of a tension of wills. On the one side is the will of God purposing, as the book of Deuteronomy says, " life and good " for men (Deut. 30:15). On the other side is the will of men, rebellious and self-seeking. Hosea states both sides of the tension of wills from which history emerges.

> When Israel was a child, I loved him,
>   and out of Egypt I called my son.
> The more I called them,
>   the more they went from me;
> they kept sacrificing to the Baals,
>   and burning incense to idols.
>
> (Hos. 11:1-2.)

Having robbed history of its vital meaning, Baalism must give the sanctions of religion to the moral and social structures raised by human pride and maintained by human sin. Having denied the reality of the Kingdom of God, it must make its home in the world. Baal casts his long and menacing shadow over modern suburbia, where the meaning of life is fulfilled in a cycle of work, barbecues, parties, and sleep, and where the ideal is to keep the wheel in perpetual motion. The most pressing danger of the big institutional church rises at the same point. Its roots go deep into the society in which it lives. It is involved in its environment, and the involvement passes all unconsciously into identification. It becomes "a community church" in the sense that the mores, the class divisions, the legal setup, and the prejudices of the community receive its stamp of approval, "God wills it." Then the church has become the temple of Baal, and needs to hear again the words of the writer to the Hebrews, "Here we have no lasting city, but we seek the city which is to come" (Heb. 13:14).

Idolatry. In the world of the prophets idolatry was almost universal. Their own strict allegiance to one God was the odd and unpopular exception to the general rule. From the Israelite levels of almost every site excavated in Palestine have come large numbers of clay figurines of the mother goddess with pronounced breasts and enlarged genital organs. These images must have been kept in the houses of ordinary Israelites as household deities, or as a kind of magical charm to ensure fertility. Their presence in Hebrew communities shows how deeply idolatrous practices had penetrated the common life of Israel.

Under such conditions the victory of monotheism over idolatry could not be won easily or quickly. At first Israel's leaders insisted only that no other gods be tolerated within their borders. Other deities might exist and be effective in their own territories, but Israel was to have no traffic with them and to offer no worship to them. The First Commandment represents this stage. "You shall have no other gods before me." (Ex. 20:3.) It contains no denial of the reality or power of the foreign gods, and is satisfied if they are kept out of the Lord's land.

The prophets went beyond what the First Commandment required. They consistently held that the Lord is the only *effective* god. They sneered at gods of wood and stone which do not move and have no life in them. By contrast with these impotent deities the God of Israel was "the living God" (Jer. 10:10). From contempt for the lifelessness and ineffectuality of pagan deities the prophets moved to the conviction that there is no reality at all corresponding to the images. They are merely the work of human hands and point to nothing beyond themselves.

What, then, is the idolater worshiping? In one form or another he is doing homage to himself, to the product of his own imagination, and to the skill of his own handiwork. Thus, in the end idolatry becomes the worship of the purely human, the veneration of man and man-made things (see Isa. 44:14-17).

The curse of idolatry in the developed prophetic meaning remains, even in the twentieth century when enlightened moderns would scorn anything so naïve as a graven image. The gods that men profess are rarely the gods to which they give allegiance, and there are many who would recite the Apostles' Creed without the flicker of an eyelash but would quickly abandon its principles if they interfered with trade. A god is anything to which man gives ultimate allegiance and beyond which he recognizes no further authority and no higher good. The person who will stop at nothing to achieve success, wealth, or social status has set up his idol and has given that kind of commitment. The person who will do anything rather than see his comfortable life disturbed, his business lost, or his family broken up is as idolatrous as the ancient Canaanite.

Security, the prestige job, the house on " Snob Hill," the supremacy of the white race, and the " American Way of Life " are human creations and human ideals. Committing himself to them, modern man is in reality worshiping himself in the guise of a man-made ideal with which he identifies himself. The prophetic polemic against idolatory is not a thing of the past. It retains its force on the modern scene, and provides the preacher with an emphasis that he must repeatedly make if the demand of Christ for ultimate allegiance to himself is to be faithfully presented. The prophetic attacks on idolatry may be read as extended commentary on the text, " You cannot serve God and mammon " (Matt. 6:24).

VII

High Lights of the Prophets

The present chapter will be memorable chiefly for its omissions. Prophetic literature contains such a wealth of homiletic material, presented with such force and insight, that it is possible to give an exegesis of only a few selected passages. The intention of the chapter is to highlight those points at which the prophet is most distinctly himself and at the same time most truly representative of the genius of the prophetic movement as a whole.

AMOS' GREAT EQUATION

Critical analysts of The Book of Amos are agreed that none of the hopeful oracles (e.g., ch. 9:11-15) can be attributed to the shepherd of Tekoa. Amos emerges from this research as a prophet whose best expectation for his people is that some few will be saved from the impending national disaster, like the prey torn from the mouth of a lion, two legs and a rag of an ear (ch. 3:12). A closer investigation of the book indicates that Amos knew of a way by which the people could escape destruction. What turns his prophecy to " darkness without light " is that he can see no possibility of his people taking that way. The truly hopeful oracles of Amos and the center of his prophetic message are to be found in ch. 5.

Amos' prophecy has one dominant theme. The corruption of the nation rises from the spirit of greed which has gained control of the political and religious leadership and has filtered down to all ranks of society. Greed produces violence, neglect for human rights, oppression of the poor, and debasement of religion. For the prophet the degeneracy of the people can be stated in a single sentence: " Justice has turned to wormwood " (ch. 5:7). Restoration of Israel's national life can come only if the missing element is restored to society, and if the people will

> Let justice roll down like water,
>   and righteousness like an everlasting stream.
>   (Ch. 5:24.)

Amos' demand for justice is grounded in the fundamental principle of Hebrew ethics — as God acts toward Israel so the Israelites should act toward one another. To the mind of the prophet the *sine qua non* of God's action is justice. His concern is to protect the weak against the power of the strong (chs. 4:1; 8:4), and he implements his purpose with perfect equity, unswayed by considerations of wealth, rank, or status. When God examines the nation he expects to find the same even-handed, impartial justice controlling the conduct of its people. To use Amos' own metaphor, justice is the plumbline in God's hand by which he measures the straightness of the national life (ch. 7:7-9). When by this standard he finds the nation crooked, its pretensions to be religious disgust him. Its sacrifices, rituals, music, processions, and solmn festivals arouse only his loathing and contempt (ch. 5:21-23).

In the light of the Christian revelation, Amos' insight is relatively small, but it may fairly be regarded as a minimum below which religion cannot be allowed to fall. As long as the big lie is tolerated, and the big swindle is regarded as good business, as long as the possession of power becomes the only necessary excuse for the abuse of power, Amos' message of justice will continue to have an essential place in Christian preaching. Amos' insistence that religion is defined by its moral content, rather than by its ritual, is a necessary corrective to too great a rejoicing over the fact that the churches are filled and the mortgages paid off. It is at this point that Amos' teaching cuts most sharply. He will not allow religion to be walled off into a corner so that its practitioners can enjoy a spiritual life and a practical life without the embarrassment of the one interfering with the other. The sphere of religion is as extensive as the range of justice, and consequently includes the whole scope of politics, economics, and social life.

The question still demanding an answer is, How can the justice requisite to the survival of the nation be produced? Taken by itself, the exhortation " Let justice roll down like water " would indicate that an effort of the will, a determined resolve to do justice, would suffice to correct the depravity of the nation. This impression is ostensibly supported by another of Amos' words:

> Seek good, and not evil,
> that you may live.
> (Ch. 5:14.)

The seeking required by the prophet, however, goes beyond a conscientious effort to do good, and involves the whole personality in an emotional reaction to good and evil.

> Hate evil, and love good.
> (Ch. 5:15.)

Love and hate cannot be commanded at will. They arise from the character that heredity, environment, and the decisions of the past have produced. Amos' apparently simple demand for justice requires for its fulfillment a change within the personality of his hearers profound enough to alter the structure of their loves and hates. Amos here faces the common dilemma of the Old Testament prophets. How is such a change possible? The only answer available to him is, " Seek the Lord and live." A return to the God who revealed himself in the events of the exodus and in the promise to the patriarchs holds out hope for that change in the national character which will release the healing force of justice and make the nation live again.

Amos' great equation contains three elements, inseparable from one another: " Let justice roll down like water " means " Seek good, and not evil," which in turn means " Seek the Lord." There is no direct road from recognition of the need for justice to the achievement of a just society. Distorted values, hatred of good and love of evil, block the direct way. Return to God and restoration by his action of a true sense of values must take place before justice, in Amos' sense of the word, can permeate society.

HOSEA AND THE FATHERHOOD OF GOD

Hosea pre-eminently is the prophet of the love of God. The best expression of his distinctive contribution to prophetic thought is not found in the much-discussed episode of his wife's harlotry but in the impassioned poem found in Hos. 11:1-9. These verses contain both the prophet's mature reflection on the meaning of Israel's history, and his pioneering statement of the fatherhood of God.

When Israel was a child, I loved him,
and out of Egypt I called him to be my son.
(V. 1.)

The starting point for Hosea, as for Old Testament thought in general, is the formative event of the exodus. The familiar elements of exodus theology are all present, directly or by implication, in Hosea's opening lines. But out of the complex of thought associated with the exodus the prophet has selected two elements which he regards as of paramount significance. God's motive in delivering the people from Egypt was love, and his saving action conferred on the nation the status of sonship.

Many nations of antiquity regarded themselves as " sons of heaven," physical descendants of one or another of the gods. Sonship for Hosea does not consist of a mingling of human and divine elements in Israel. The status of sons was conferred on the people in a historical act by which God adopted them as his children. It was conferred in love and was to be confirmed by obedience. The characteristics of the father are love and election; the responsibilities of the son, obedience and service.

How did historic Israel respond to the duties of sonship?

I, indeed, called to them,
and they went away from my presence.
They sacrificed to the baals,
and to graven images they burned incense.
(V. 2.)

Hosea's condemnation of Israel is an accurate report of historical facts and also a commentary on the decisive element in human nature. God may offer sonship to man, but man is not compelled to accept the offer. Such is his radical freedom that he may spurn the love of God and attach himself to a master more easily served and more attractive to his fickle mind. However, a religious vacuum does not exist. Man must have some object to serve and to venerate. If it is not the Lord, then it will be the baals.

God's reaction to the apostasy of his people is the persevering continuance of his love for them.

> But it was I [i.e., not the baals] who taught
>> Ephraim how to walk,
> taking them in my arms;
>> but they did not know that it was I who healed
>> them.
>
> (V. 3.)

Hosea interpreted the early sins of Israel — the episode of the golden calf, and the "murmurings" of the wilderness period — as the stumbling of a child learning to walk. The kindly father God taught it how to control its erratic steps, and when the child stumbled and fell, he took it in his arms and comforted it in its injuries. But the tragedy of Israel was that she did not know this. The nation attributed her success to her own strength or to the power of the baals. Even at the late date in her history when Hosea was preaching, the nation had not sufficiently understood the nature of her God to see that the guiding hand was his, the support was from him, and the power was his gift.

The prophet now abruptly changes the metaphor from father to ox drover.

> With humane cords I led them along,
>> with the ropes of love,
> And I became to them as one who lifts the yoke
>> from their jaws,
> I stooped to them and fed them.
>
> (V. 4.)

God's way with his people was to place responsibility upon them in order to bring them to sonship along the path of service. The nation had come under stern discipline, and was like a team of oxen toiling up a stiff grade with a loaded cart. But the burdens that the people had to bear were also the devices of love. The cords by which God drew them along were humane cords, and the ropes that bound them to the load were ropes of love. When the load became too heavy, God was there to lighten it, to loosen the yoke and to feed the tired oxen.

Hosea's use of the double metaphor is a valuable reminder to the preacher of the limitations inherent in the metaphor of God as father. Father and son are on terms of too-near equality. The fatherhood of God needs to be supplemented by metaphors capable of expressing God's otherness from man and the absolute nature of his demands upon mankind. Hosea selected for this purpose the somewhat repellent figure of the ox drover forcing his beasts along a steep road, but in principle and intent the metaphor is not different from that of the shepherd guiding and protecting the sheep (see p. 16).

Ephraim responded neither to the God who took them in his arms, nor to the God who put them under a kindly yoke. They were children who despised their father, and oxen who kicked at the goad. If the ox refuses to pull, there comes a time when the drover must take up the whip. When the father's every attempt to lead, educate, and save his children has been rejected, he must with sorrow resort to punishment. In a universe ruled by a just God, persistent, unrepented sin must receive its appropriate judgment.

The prophet foresaw two possible disasters threatening the nation. He did not attempt to say which would be its ultimate fate.

> They will return to Egypt,
> or Assyria will rule over them,
> for they have refused to return.
> (V. 5.)

In either case the result of rejecting the love of God is slavery. Hosea's thought is again in harmony with that of the New Testament, the difference being that, whereas the Old Testament prophet contemplates political slavery for the nation, the New Testament writers think in terms of slavery to sin and the powers of death. The reasoning is, however, the same in both Testaments. Liberty is to be found only in the status of sonship. Outside this saving relationship, slavery is the rule of life.

The text of the next two verses is hopelessly corrupt, and there are ten ways of construing it. The only certainty is that the prophet accuses the nation of shameful disregard for the love of God.

> A sword shall whirl about in their cities,
> and shall consume their branches,
> and devour their forts.
> My people are swung toward rebellion against
> me;
> they are destined for the yoke [of slavery],
> and none shall remove it. (Vs. 6-7.)

How does God feel at the prospect of bringing a sword against his people? The prophet presumes to tell his readers. God is consumed with an overwhelming sympathy for his suffering people. No sin or rebellion of theirs can quench the flow of the divine mercy.

> How can I give you up, O Ephraim,
> how let you go, O Israel?
> How can I make you like Admah,
> how treat you like Zeboim?

My heart is turned against me,
  my compassion grows warm and tender
I will not carry out the heat of my anger,
I will not turn to destroy Ephraim,
  for I am God and not man,
  the Holy One in your midst.
I will not come to destroy.

(Vs. 8-9.)

These verses are anthropomorphism carried to its fullest extent. God is pictured as torn between two conflicting emotions: fierce anger at the apostasy of his people and equally violent pity at the destruction that overshadows them. The struggle between wrath and compassion is fierce, but compassion prevails. The punishment about to fall on Israel will not result in total destruction, but will be the means of national restoration and renewal. Through the disaster of foreign conquest, Israel will be recalled to sonship.

Just when the reader feels that anthropomorphism has gone too far in depicting God as the victim of his own emotions, the prophet shows that he is aware of the danger. Explicitly he denies the intention of equating human and divine: "I am God and not man." How could the prophet describe God's reaction to apostasy except in terms of human anger and compassion? Yet he would not say that he had captured in human language the reality of God's inner life. God remains "the Holy One," the mighty, awe-inspiring Other, whose impenetrable mystery defies all attempts to pry into its secrets.

Hosea's Holy One is different from the holy ones of the pagan world. He is in the midst of his people. The terrifying power of the holy has been brought down from the sky and out of the streams, trees, and woods, where primitive man looked for it, and has taken up its abode with man. It is no longer arbitrary brute force, breaking out against human society in meaningless destruction. The holiness of Hosea's God — that which differentiates him from man — is his compassion and love, by which he guards, instructs, and leads his people. If he punishes, it is in order to redeem.

Hosea's meditation on the fatherhood of God provides a framework within which the Christian can examine and interpret the work of Christ. Man's destiny is sonship with God, a status made possible initially by the gracious call of God, and continued by the education and disciplining of his children in love. Rejection of this status is slavery. Seen from the point of view of the rebel, this is the destructive operation of the wrath of God. Viewed from God's side, it is the divine compassion proceeding from the love of God and seeking to redeem and restore.

Isaiah — The Work of the Spirit

The conclusion that the work of God in man has a specifiable, ethical, and even political, result is explicit in Amos and Hosea. The former dreamed of a just society, free of brutality and aggression, and founded upon the justice of God. The latter envisaged a community of the children of God in which the father's love and compassion controlled the behavior of the sons. For both prophets the precondition of the new order was a *direct* return of the nation to the God of Israel.

Like his contemporaries in the prophetic movement, Isaiah of Jerusalem hoped for a new era beyond the confusion and struggle of his own lifetime. He wrote of the age to come as a time of universal harmony when violence and fear would be totally eliminated, so that

The wolf shall dwell with the lamb,
  and the leopard shall lie down with the kid,
and the calf and the lion and the fatling to-
    gether,
  and a little child shall lead them.

                                    (Isa. 11:6.)

Unlike Amos and Hosea, Isaiah saw the new era, not as
the result of a direct return to the Lord by Israel, but as
mediated to Israel through the Messiah of the line of David
(vs. 1-3). A new character, corresponding to the needs of
the new age, would be produced in the Messiah by the action of the Spirit of the Lord, and would be transmitted
through him to Israel.

The form of Isaiah's call to prophesy may in part be responsible for his insistence on the necessity of a mediator
of the divine righteousness. He saw "the Lord, high and
lifted up" (ch. 6:1). In Isaiah's vision the exalted God
spoke, but did not act. He dispatched a seraph to cleanse
the prophet's lips, and commissioned Isaiah himself to be
the messenger to Israel. The pouring out of the Spirit of the
Lord on Israel in the age to come would likewise be achieved
through a messenger of God's choosing.

The endowments of the Spirit by which the Messiah is
equipped to usher in the age of harmony are three in number, each member of the triad consisting of two complementary qualities: (1) wisdom and understanding, (2) counsel and might, and (3) knowledge and the fear of the Lord
(ch. 11:2).

In the Hebrew language, "wisdom" means primarily the
ability to accomplish what one sets out to do. The desired
goal may be morally bad and socially destructive, but if a
person has the skill to reach it, he is a "wise man." Thus
when Amnon wished to seduce his beautiful half sister, he

sought the advice of a "wise man" to instruct him in the art of seduction (II Sam. 13:3).

Since wisdom is morally ambiguous, it must be supplemented by understanding (better, "discernment"), that is, the power to decide in a given set of circumstances what is worth doing.

"Counsel," the ability to form an intelligent and workable plan, is mere frustration in the absence of the "might" required to carry the plan into effect. The capacity to make a clear decision amidst the ambiguities of an existing situation and the power to bring the decision to reality are indispensable to the Messiah in his task of inaugurating the new order.

Thus far the gifts of the Spirit may be used either for good or for evil. Wisdom can be distorted to evil ends, and counsel may be used to oppose the purpose of God. The prophet, therefore, climaxed his account of the Messiah's attributes with two qualities that guaranteed the orientation of the others toward the service of God. The life of the Messiah would be lived in that close personal fellowship which in the Biblical language is called the "knowledge of God." But the Messiah's nearness to God is not the familiarity that breeds contempt. It is knowledge tempered and informed with the fear of the Lord. It is nearness in reverential awe to the majestic presence of the Heavenly King. The Messiah will not rejoice in the exercise of his unlimited power. Rather, his joy will be the humble worship of his God. "His delight shall be in the fear of the Lord." (Isa. 11:3.)

The presence in the Messiah of these gifts of the Spirit will make them prevail in the nation under his rule. As the divine gifts permeate the structure of society, the age of harmony will be ushered in, in which

They shall not hurt or destroy
in all my holy mountain;
for the earth shall be full of the knowledge of
the Lord
as the waters cover the sea.

(Isa. 11:9.)

The promise-fulfillment relationship between the Testaments is nowhere more clearly in evidence than in the Messianic prophecies of Isaiah. The substance of these prophecies offers the Christian preacher both a challenge and a stimulus in his preaching of the Messiahship of Jesus Christ.

JEREMIAH — THE NATURE OF TRUST

Like his three great predecessors, Jeremiah knew that the salvation of Israel depended upon her relationship with God. Like them, he too had much to say about the activity of God and the nature of man. But in a way unique among the prophets he concentrated on the middle term between God and man, the human response to the divine activity. As a prophet, Jeremiah was rejected by the people to whom he came to preach. He was tormented by doubts of his own prophetic vocation, and precisely because the bond between himself and God was so often nearly broken, its nature and preservation became for him a matter of supreme importance. The one word which to Jeremiah's mind best described the heart of the divine-human relationship was "trust." This word (Hebrew, *bātāh*) basically means "to throw oneself forward." It connotes an unqualified abandonment of the self to the revealed love and mercy of God, an almost reckless throwing of oneself on the divine mercy and protection in complete confidence that it will be there, and that it will be able to sustain the one who thus unreservedly commits himself to it.

This concept of trust occupied so central a place in the thought of Jeremiah that he represented it as the secret of salvation or destruction, life or death. There are two realms in which trust can be placed: the Lord, or man and man-made devices. To the second of these, Jeremiah gave the name "flesh." The important issues of life are settled by whether trust is given to the Lord or to flesh.

> Cursed is the man who trusts in man
> and makes flesh his arm . . . .
> Blessed is the man who trusts in the Lord,
> whose trust is the Lord.
>
> (Jer. 17:5, 7.)

The cursing and blessing of these verses are not punitive or rewarding acts of God, but are qualities of life issuing from the nature of the trust by which life is sustained. A "blessed" life is one of well-rounded completeness. The full capacities of the personality are developed and its deepest needs satisfied. A "cursed" life is lonely, unrealized, and unfulfilled. The difference between the two kinds of existence seemed to Jeremiah like that between a shrub struggling to survive in the parched and barren wilderness, and a tree, green and laden with fruit, growing beside a stream. The desert-growing shrub, the man who trusts in man, puts forth its roots of trust but finds that they finger out only in the dry sand, finding no life-sustaining water. He may do well enough in good times when the air is cool and the refreshing rain falls, but under the merciless beat of the sun the shrub deprived of water shrivels and dies.

Every financial depression proves the accuracy of Jeremiah's analogy. The suicide of men who have trusted in wealth and who, when it is gone, have literally lost everything is only an especially dramatic illustration of the prophet's far-reaching principle, the operation of which can be seen throughout the entire range of human experience. The tree "planted by water" (ch. 17:8) likewise puts out the roots of its trust, but they reach to an authentic source of nourishment, and along them flows a life-giving power. Jeremiah singled out for special notice two outstanding qualities of the man whose trust is the Lord. The first is his staying power. The burden and heat of the day which kill the wilderness shrub cannot destroy him. He is not indifferent to the environment around him, but he is not dependent on it for his existence. Because the sustenance of his life does not fail in the time of trouble, he has no fear of its coming and no anxiety as to his power to sustain its impact (v. 8). In the second place, his life is a productive one. He does not cease to bear fruit (v. 8). In no small measure these two qualities constitute the "blessedness" of the life founded on trust in the Lord. Such a life is secure within itself and a blessing to others.

The metaphor of the two trees is only one graphic expression of a theme to which Jeremiah often returned, clothing the single basic idea with a richness of metaphor which only the imagination of a poet of the first rank could command.

Jeremiah contrasted the cisterns made by the people for themselves, attractive in appearance but broken and leaking, with "the fountain of living waters" whom the nation had forsaken (ch. 2:13). He castigated Israel for calling her idols of wood and stone "father" and appealing to them for deliverance (v. 27). He compared the nation to a bride who, as soon as the memory of the wedding began to fade, took to the road in search of other lovers (vs. 32-37). He attacked confidence in armies and treaties, in wealth, in wis-

dom, and in the formal practice of religion, always returning to the position that life is essentially a matter of trust.
Any foundation of trust other than the living God is sure
to fail, and to precipitate the life established upon it into
frustration and disaster.

Jeremiah's treatment of the theme of trust opens an
avenue by which the Christian may approach the New
Testament concept of faith. Modern Christianity treats faith
casually. It is the subject of theological discussion (as it
ought to be) and the battleground of interdenominational
debates, but the sense of urgency in its proclamation is missing. Jeremiah was never casual. He knew that not many to-
morrows remained for the people to whom he preached and
he was keenly aware of the momentous issues that are decided by trust. The Christian preacher cannot permit the
faith that he proclaims to be represented as less urgent or
less decisive than Jeremiah's trust.

EZEKIEL — THE SIGNIFICANCE OF THE TEMPLE

By concentrating on the ethical demands made by God
upon Israel, the prophets left an unresolved ambiguity concerning the place of the sacrificial and ritual elements in
the national religion. Sometimes they appear to call for a
reformation of the cult, sometimes to regard it as a matter of
no importance, and sometimes to demand its complete
abolition.

The ambiguity is most clearly evident in the prophetic
attitude toward the Temple. The psalms reveal the high
place that popular piety gave to the city of David and the
place of worship on Mt. Zion.

> The joy of the whole earth is Mt. Zion.
>
> (Ps. 48:2.)

The Lord loves the gates of Zion
more than all the dwelling places of Jacob.
(Ps. 87:2.)

Isaiah had predicated his successful prophecy that Jerusalem would not be captured by the Assyrians on the assumption that the Lord would not let his dwelling place
fall into the hands of pagan invaders. This prophecy, spoken
in a particular situation, hardened into the dogma of the
absolute inviolability of the Temple. As long as it stood in
Jerusalem, the city could never be the victim of conquest.
Jeremiah thus found his predictions of doom faced by the
flippant rejoinder, " The Temple of the Lord is with us "
(Jer. 7:4). This was all that needed to be said to counteract
the prophet's blasphemous insistence that Jerusalem would
be utterly destroyed. Jeremiah's reply to his critics was a historical one. Shiloh had been the chief sacred place in ancient
times, but God had permitted the Philistines to reduce it to
rubble. Jerusalem could expect no better fate, if it continued
to use the existence of the Temple as an insurance policy to
protect it from the consequences of its own sins. Trust in
the Temple as an institution was no substitute for trust in,
and obedience to, God (Jer., ch. 7).

Jeremiah's attitude faced the nation's confidence in the
inviolability of the Temple with a flat denial, but it left the
question of the Lord's relationship to the place of worship
unanswered. To this problem Ezekiel addressed himself.
For him the Temple was the place where the " glory " of
God dwelt; that is, the place where he revealed his authority over the national life. As long as the divine authority
was resident in the Temple the sacred place was beyond the
reach of the foreign conqueror. National rejection of the authority of God, however, would cause God to remove his
glory from the sacred place. It then became an empty shell,

a building without a soul, and lay open to the attack and destruction of the invader. It was, therefore, a decisive moment in Ezekiel's prophecy when "the glory of the Lord went up from the midst of the city, and stood upon the mountain which is on the east side of the city" (Ezek. 11:23). With its army still intact, Jerusalem had, by the withdrawal of the divine authority from its midst, been reduced to defenselessness. In an equally momentous vision the prophet saw the return of the glory of God to fill the restored Temple after the period of exile in Babylon was over (ch. 43:1-5).

Ezekiel thus permits no sentimentalizing of the place of worship. The "church in the valley by the wildwood," with its childhood associations and its "clear ringing bell," may titilate the fancy and evoke a spurious loyalty, but it represents only the peripheral attraction of the church. The church exists primarily as the place where God's authority is declared and acknowledged. Unless this transaction takes place within its walls, it has no more claim to the title of sacred than a national sports shrine.

Since the presence of the glory of God gives permanence and value to the place of worship, Ezekiel's picture of the divine glory is of more than ordinary interest in his prophecy. The vision of God's glory (Ezek., ch. 1) which the prophet saw beside the river Chebar in Babylon was a spectacular and awe-inspiring sight. Out of the distance across the flat plains of the Euphrates a great cloud, its top lost in the blue of the sky, came rolling and swaying toward the prophet, spouting lightning flashes and echoing with a long roll of thunder as it came. Within the cloud were four huge double wheels, the rims glaring and gleaming with innumerable eyes. Above the wheels towered four creatures — part bird, part animal, part man, and part angel. Above that, curved a great sapphire dome reflecting blue light, like the cold surface of an ice field. Above the dome and far removed from the prophet was a huge throne on which sat something that resembled a human figure, clothed in fire from the waist down. The whole gigantic chariot rolled forward irresistibly with the stately but terrifying movement of a huge machine, a kind of celestial seventy-five-ton tank, crushing its inevitable way onward.

The vision was spectacular enough in its own right, but it becomes even more impressive when it is realized that the prophet is painting a picture of the universe. At first it strikes us as bizarre and repellent because it represents the universe as a mighty, irresistible machine.

One of the names of Vishnu, the Preserver of the Indian pantheon, is Jagannath or Juggernaut, the "Lord of the World." In the city of Puri every year a great procession moves through the streets. At its center and focal point is a huge wagon bearing a tall wooden tower on which is placed the image of Juggernaut, seated on his throne. The Lord of the Universe travels through the streets of Puri in his throne car like Ezekiel's God on the celestial chariot, and the crowds prostrate themselves before him with cries of "Great God Juggernaut." Both the prophet and the theologians of India conceive the world as a great machine.

Although we may call this primitive superstition, if we mock Juggernaut we are mocking ourselves and our civilization. The world of wheels, the remorseless machine, is what our society has become for many of our fellow human beings — a soulless mechanism, rolling mercilessly past and over human lives, caring nothing for human hopes and human dreams but simply grinding on its way, blind and heedless.

Twentieth-century culture is in danger of losing its humanity. Its proper symbol is not the human being, but the intermeshing cogs of a transmission or the electric spark jumping across the gap between two electrodes. We have come so far along this way that we confuse progress with gain in technical know-how. We speak, without a blush of shame, about the citizens of our country as " our greatest natural resource," as if a person were to be used and exploited like ore from a mine. Our colleges and universities have too often turned themselves into education mills, " turning out," as the ghastly phrase has it, graduates with diplomas but without scholarship. The churches, which ought to be the prophetic voices speaking for the dignity and worth of the individual, have not infrequently had their voices silenced by success. Some now prefer to be spiritual tranquilizers crying " Peace, peace " when there is no peace. Such churches are architecturally and liturgically correct prisons for the incarceration of the Holy Spirit, and servants of the great god Juggernaut.

The prophet Ezekiel was realist enough to know that the machine is with us as a permanent feature of our lives. No amount of idle wishing for the return of the mythical day of the common man, which in fact never was on sea or land, will change the fact that the world and the church roll machinelike on their way. What the prophet was deeply concerned to show is the way in which the machine may be given a soul and a life; so it will no longer be remorseless and dehumanizing, but will express the dream and the hope, will have room in the machinery for the humane and the joyful, will make men and will not crush them in the wheels. Ezekiel's answer is twofold. In his vision of the great throne chariot, the all-important thing is that God sits enthroned above it. " Above the firmament was the likeness of a throne." Here is what saves the machine from soullessness. Under what authority does it move? Under the authority of chance, under the authority of science, under the authority of humanity, under the authority of the bishop or the presbytery? If any of these is the answer, mankind is lost and the machine will destroy him. But the answer is none of these. The universe moves under the authority of God. The machines that man makes will find their souls only as they too are dedicated to the service of the living God.

In Ezekiel's vision there was another feature that robbed the machine of its inhumanity. "The spirit of the living creatures was in the wheels." The wheels have no meaning or direction in themselves. They turn, but their turning is destructive and dehumanizing unless the Spirit of God is present in them, guiding their motion and giving it purpose. This Spirit of God, which moves the machine forward on its way, is strikingly referred to by Ezekiel as the spirit of the living creatures. It is a humane spirit, a spirit of grace, kindliness, and love. The glory of God for Ezekiel is his world-ruling and world-guiding power, the presence of which means that the human being lives in a world in which he is known and understood, and not in the midst of the grinding cogs of a soulless machine.

Ezekiel's response to the vision of the glory of God was to fall upon his face in reverence and worship. In this supine position he heard the divine voice commanding him, "Son of man, stand upon your feet, and I will speak with you." These words have become the basis of numerous exhortations to Christians to rise up and spring into action. The word of God, we are told, will not come to a man unless he assumes the position of a true human being, erect, alert, ready for immediate action in the name of God. Such humanistic pleas can be supported by Ezekiel's vision only if the words that immediately follow the divine command are deliberately ignored. "The Spirit entered into me and set me upon my feet." If Ezekiel assumes the stance of a human being in God's presence, it is because God empowers him to do so.

The same thought reappears in even more pointed form in the famous vision of the Valley of Dry Bones (Ezek. 37:1-14). The bones, the dry and hopeless wreckage of Israelite society, cannot live again unless the word of God enters into them and gives them life. The Negro spiritual has helped perpetuate the misunderstanding that "Ezekiel connected them dry bones." He did not! They were gathered together, covered with flesh, and made living men by the action of God. Nevertheless, the error persists that the church can save men, the minister win souls, and the pastor heal the wounds of the human spirit. It is to our shame that we do not understand our Bible better. The church neither converts nor heals. The sovereign Lord of the church is the Savior and the Physician.

What, then, is the church? Its function is no different from the function of Ezekiel, the prophet. It is to prophesy to the dry bones and say, "O dry bones, hear the word of the Lord." It is a witnessing community whose every action points, not to itself and its own authority, but beyond itself to the authority of God.

A church understanding itself in the way indicated by Ezekiel, as a community witnessing to the authority of God, an authority that it has itself acknowledged and by which it lives, is the instrument of God for the restoration and healing of society. To this theme Ezekiel devoted the last nine chapters of his prophecy. As usual with him, the style is turgid and repetitious, but he makes three points unmistakably clear. The place of worship forms the organizing center of restored Israel. About it the tribes grouped themselves in precise order. The details of the arrangement are laboriously given, but the basic idea is clear. The glory of God gives structure, order, coherence, and unity.

A stream of water flowed from beneath the altar of the restored Temple, bringing life to the entire land and providing it with a new fertility and beauty. The beneficent effect of the water was not confined to the land, which had all along been productive. It rolled on into the wasteland and transformed it into an oasis of grass and fruit trees. Its flow purified the salt waters of the Dead Sea, which thereafter teemed with fish.

Ezekiel's vision of the re-established place of worship where the glory of God came to take up its residence is a powerful statement of the function of the church in society. If the church understands itself rightly, it can give order and unity in place of chaos and division. It can rejuvenate the life of its own people. It can reclaim the waste and desolate places in individual life and in society. This is a possibility, however, only as the church renounces the claim to be, itself, the healing waters and permits itself to be the channel through which they flow. This in turn depends on the church's willingness to take what appears to be the humble and unimpressive role of witness to the authority of God, the divine glory, which is in it, but which it can claim neither to possess nor to control.

DEUTERO-ISAIAH — THE ONE GOD

The forty-fifth chapter of Isaiah is a poem worthy to stand beside the fortieth chapter (see p. 18). In it the writer rings the changes on the idea of pure monotheism. Six times in twenty-one verses the prophet repeats his credo in slightly

variant forms, " I am the Lord, and there is no other " (Isa.
45:5, 6, 14, 18, 21, 22).

Monotheism is not, however, valued by the prophet as a
theoretical hypothesis. Once belief in one God is stated, it
brings with it a chain of consequences for the one who pro-
fesses this faith. In the Deutero-Isaiah's poem, interwoven
with the monotheistic creed, the secondary themes of creation (vs. 7, 8, 12, 18), providence (vs. 13, 14, 16, 19), and
especially salvation (vs. 8, 15, 17, 21) persistently recur.

The exclusive nature of monotheistic religion (" There is
none beside me ") excludes all other power from any share
in genuine creative activity. Light and darkness, weal and
woe, the earth and persons who live upon it have their
origin and reason for existence in the wisdom of God. It
follows, then, that " only in the Lord are righteousness and
strength " (v. 24). The restless human quest for power and
goodness, for a just society in a remade world, has its goal
in God. In the Old Testament vocabulary the verb " create "
(*bārâ*) is used only with God as subject. In spite of his
artistic pretensions, man is never a creator. Therefore, *re-*
creation, rebirth, restoration are likewise exclusively divine
activities.

As Deutero-Isaiah perceived and taught, there is an inti-
mate connection between monotheism, creation, and salvation. The one God, uniquely the creator, is "a righteous
God and a savior " (v. 21). In this formula, Deutero-Isaiah
presented exiled Israel with the most theologically convincing argument for her ultimate restoration. The creator, and
he alone, is able to re-create the scattered nation and restore
her common life to wholeness and health. The historical
occasion that called forth the prophecy of Deutero-Isaiah
belongs to the past, but the implications of his monotheism
on both the positive and negative sides retain their validity.

Wherever salvation is sought by other means than the activity of God, the spirit of idolatry is at work. But wherever belief in one God, the sole creative power in the universe, is a vital faith, it impels men to abandon every attempt to save themselves and to realize that their one hope of salvation is with him.

This exclusive concentration on God alone as the sole ground of deliverance enables the Christian to accept the immense improbability that a carpenter of Nazareth is the Son of God and the Savior of mankind. Logic is against it, but logic is not capable of saving the logician. Jesus Christ, met in the personal encounter of faith, brings with him, and indeed is himself the creative power of God, the power, as Paul says, " unto salvation."

The monotheism of Deutero-Isaiah led him to draw an absolute contrast between the religion of Israel and that of the pagan nations. Their worship represented religion in reverse, a mockery of the genuine relationship between God and man. Irony and wry humor are combined in the prophet's description of the Babylonian New Year festival (Isa., ch. 46). In this, the most solemn and impressive ritual of the Neo-Babylonian empire, the Hebrew prophet saw his analysis of the nature of paganism dramatically confirmed.

From the northern walls of Babylon to the temple of Marduk, a distance of one thousand yards, ran a walled-in roadway over twenty feet wide, paved with limestone flags and flanked on either side by sixty huge lions portrayed in enameled brick. This magnificent road was the triumphal way along which at the New Year festival the statues of the gods were brought in triumph through the city to their temples to be enthroned for another year of rule. Huge creaking carts, pulled by straining beasts and men, carried the massive idols along the processional road. This spectacle of human beings and animals hauling their deities laboriously through the streets was for the prophet typical of a religion that becomes a burden on its followers, of a god who must be propped up, supported, and borne along by the toil of his worshipers.

Modern religion is free of the physical burden of idols, but not of the type of religion which the prophet was caricaturing. Christianity is sometimes represented as a heavy and a weary weight. It takes numerous joyless forms in which the Christian is called upon to bear up under the stern pressure of inexorable duty and is given to understand that the survival of his fath depends upon his efforts to sustain it. Outside Christianity the contemporary world provides innumerable illustrations of men, like Atlas, trying to hold up the sky. Having discovered the cure for the ills of the age, they find that their secular religion, far from healing, becomes an idol resting on their shoulders and pressing them down. Even pleasure, pursued either as an escape from the responsibilities of life or as an end in itself, has this same deceptive quality. It begins as the chariot on which the hedonist will ride into happiness; but before the day is over, the positions are reversed and the lover of pleasure becomes the beast of burden, carrying his broken-down vehicle on his back.

Deutero-Isaiah contended that no god was worthy of consideration who needed to be shored up and carried along by his worshipers. The God of Israel has no need for such human support. He bore and sustained his human children from cradle to grave.

> I have made, and I will bear;
> I will carry and I will save.
>
> (Isa. 46:4.)

At a single stroke the man of faith is relieved of the odious necessity of holding up God by his efforts. When he rejects the idols and comes face to face with the Creator God of the prophet, man recognizes that his own effort is not competent even to sustain himself. If he is to move through life purposefully and constructively, it will be because he has relinquished his claim to walk alone and has allowed himself to be carried by God.

The Biblical revelation is never kind to the independent spirit. Most of us would rather walk by ourselves and would like to think of God as always nearby to lend a helping hand over the rough spots. A "God is my copilot" complex is deeply ingrained in human nature. We hold the controls most of the time, but it is reassuring to know that there is an unseen Other in the cabin ready to take over and fly *our* course for us. The rigid monotheism of the prophet leaves no room for another creative or saving power beyond God or instead of God, and no halfway house exists between autonomy and dependence upon the Creator.

The realization of this truth, like the acknowledgment of sin, is a tremendous release. The necessity of discipline and sustained effort remains. Life is neither a bed of roses nor an irresponsible oblivion to the world. However, man is no longer compelled to regard what he does as the final reality in human history, nor to feel on his shoulders the weight of saving the world. He will work, and even suffer, joyfully, since the consequences are in the ultimate charge of God. He can fail without despair, since his failure may be useful to God. He can succeed without pride, because success is God's work. In the varied experiences that lie between the poles of success and failure he is upheld by God, led by God, corrected by God, and used by God. The life of joy and hope made possible by the consciousness of being borne by God constituted for Deutero-Isaiah the essence of religion. The Christian knows the identical experience in its fullness by his fellowship with Jesus Christ within the community of the church.

VIII

The Psalter

The Hebrew psalms present the preacher with an embarrassment of riches. Every major theme of Old Testament thought enters into the composition of these lyrics. Scholars too have found much in the Psalter to stimulate their research, so that psalm studies is one of the most active fields in modern Old Testament scholarship. With so much to choose from, it is necessary to select a single pathway through the psalms and to pursue it resolutely, ignoring a good deal of material that would have been equally valuable had another way been chosen.

The hermeneutical principle developed in Chapter I, by which the viewpoint toward the Old Testament is developed out of the New Testament revelation leads naturally to selection of the theme of sin and salvation. There is justification for this choice in the psalms themselves. Literary analysis of the psalm types shows that songs of lamentation far outnumber hymns of praise or of thanksgiving.

THE PERIL OF INNOCENCE

The psalmists frequently repel Christian readers by their outspoken hatred of their enemies and their insistent demand for vengeance. Almost all Protestant collections of responsive readings include Ps. 137, but invariably without the last verse. The haunting beauty of the opening lines,

> By the waters of Babylon,
> there we sat down and wept,
> when we remembered Zion,

is marred by the open vindictiveness of the concluding couplet,

> Happy shall he be who takes your little ones
> And dashes them against the rock!

Psalm 31 contains a moving statement of trust in the goodness of God:

> I trust in thee, O Lord,
> I say, " Thou art my God."
> My times are in thy hand;
>   deliver me from the hand of my enemies and
>   persecutors!
> Let thy face shine on thy servant;
>   save me in thy steadfast love!

(Vs. 14-16.)

Immediately thereafter, the psalmist calls for the destruction of the insolent liars who are his enemies:

> Let the wicked be put to shame,
>   let them go dumbfounded to Sheol.
> Let the lying lips be dumb,
>   which speak insolently against the righteous
>   in pride and contempt.

(Vs. 17-18.)

Because of the clearly sub-Christian nature of these cries for vengeance many preachers ignore them or flee for refuge to the Sermon on the Mount. In either case, the value of these psalms is lost to the Christian preacher because of failure to face honestly the problem of their presence in the Bible and to inquire after the "why" of the psalmists' vindictive spirit.

The attitude of the psalmists was not the result of perversity or cruelty. It was an integral part of their religious understanding. To appreciate why the psalmists' religion required vengeance is to show by contrast why the gospel implies forgiveness.

In every psalm where the vengeful spirit is dominant it goes hand in hand with an expressed conviction of innocence. The enemy belongs to the ranks of the damned, but the psalmist is one of the righteous. He asks that God judge him " according to the integrity that is in me " (Ps. 7:8). In words that are almost a challenge to God, he declares, " If thou testest me, thou wilt find no wickedness in me " (Ps. 17:3). He insists, " I have trusted in the Lord without wavering " (Ps. 26:1). Contrasting himself with " bloodthirsty men, men in whose hands are evil devices," he asserts, " As for me, I walk in my integrity; . . . my foot stands on level ground " (Ps. 26:9-12).

Vindictiveness and the sense of innocence belong together as effect and cause. Consciousness of one's own moral adequacy and near-perfection is as dangerous and destructive as any entry in the long catalog of spiritual perils. As seen in the psalms, it exerts its baleful effect in three directions.

1. The psalmist equates his enemies with the enemies of God. Anyone who has the temerity to attack an innocent man, one who trusts solely in the Lord, must by definition be hostile to God. In destroying the oppressors of the psalm-

ist, God is snuffing out his own enemies. The cry for vengeance is, thus, a calling upon God to avenge himself.

The insidious danger here is that the "innocent" may, perhaps unconsciously, equate his cause with God's purpose and himself, in effect, with God. He cannot come under judgment, for God has already declared him "not guilty." His enemies (i.e., God's enemies) can expect only destruction, and prayer for their speedy demise is in reality an expression of the will of God.

Pity is too tender a plant to grow in this frigid air. Desire for the redemption of the enemy is out of the question. It would be impious, and in a sense blasphemous, to hope for anything but his destruction. Accordingly, the man is blessed who "dashes their little ones on the rock."

There is no one more unbending and implacable than the person who knows that he is righteous, and that his righteousness has been sealed by divine approval. The history of the church has been repeatedly marred by the cruelty of men, secure in their goodness, who identified their own welfare with the will of God. The Inquisition burned the enemies of the established order because they were enemies of God and a danger to the church. But the Inquisition is only a remote and extreme example of what happens daily in interpersonal relationships. The bitterest family and community quarrels arise from feelings of injured innocence, and become more and more nearly irreconcilable in proportion to the strength of that feeling. The hope of reconciliation begins when someone in the situation has the grace to feel guilty.

2. When the "innocent" comes under persecution or hardship, his resentment may not be directed toward man alone but may be turned against God. If the Ruler of the universe lets such a good man as he suffer, he must be

either an unjust tyrant or a being indifferent to the claims of righteousness. The vigor with which some psalmists try to prod God into action by their prayers reveals an impatience with his failure to recognize their goodness, and an implicit accusation that he has ceased to care about their plight. " Rouse thyself! Why sleepest thou, O Lord?" (Ps. 44:23.)

The classic case of resentment against God is not in the Psalter but in The Book of Job. All the eloquence of Job's "friends" and the combined force of their arguments and sarcasm cannot shake his assurance that he is innocent before God and man. In ch. 31 he recites a list of virtues that runs to forty verses (the best single statement of Hebrew ethical ideals in the Old Testament), and pronounces himself blameless on every count. In his lowest moments Job accuses God of harrying him, pursuing him, and by the exercise of arbitrary brute force robbing him of his right. He is not delivered from this bitter mood until God speaks to him from the whirlwind. Then his vision is lifted beyond himself, and what is due to him, to the contemplation of the wisdom and majesty of God.

Most Christians are tarred with the same brush as the psalmists. They are, to quote themselves, " by no means perfect," but they are good people trying to do their best, and they expect some protection and reward in return for their efforts. When trouble comes they want to know, Why did God let this happen to *me?* But, then: Why not to me? If disease attacks my neighbor's body, why should it spare me? If death comes to the sons of other men, why not to mine? God does not turn pain away from the Christian as a reward for his obedience. Rather, he empowers the Christian to use his suffering as part of his redemptive witness. Only a false interpretation of righteousness which makes it the ground of special reward can bring God under indictment because of the suffering of a good man.

3. The third consequence of a sense of innocence is self-righteousness and contempt for others. The " innocent " are a select group, and they know it. Persons outside their number are moral failures, lesser beings, deficient in spiritual muscular development. The " innocent " are thus led to think of themselves as a religious master-race, superior to all who fall short of their rigid specifications. Their attitude of " innocence " cuts them off from the very people whom their religion requires them to serve. The outsiders are repelled by the hard faces and the obvious contempt with which the innocent regard them as sinners. The insiders are prevented from going out to them for fear of jeopardizing their innocence by contact with sinners. If the " innocent " win converts, it is because of desire to become part of the favored few; and if they serve, it is by condescension, not by love.

Jesus was not uttering a moral platitude when he concluded the parable of the unprofitable servant with the words, "When you have done all that is commanded you, say, 'We are unworthy servants; we have only done what was our duty'" (Luke 17:10). His words are a warning against the sense of worthiness and achievement which breeds contempt and issues in cruelty. When the Christian has done *all,* he has still no shred of claim to reward or favor and no reason to hold his head higher than his fellows.

The consciousness of sin, often regarded as psychologically dangerous, is in fact a tremendous release from the burden of sustaining an impossible position of innocence. The realization of sin can be debilitating only if it is an unrelieved knowledge of guilt, with no hope of deliverance or forgiveness. When, however, the sense of sin leads to recognition of dependence on the mercies of God and to an appeal for forgiveness, it is transmuted into a liberating experience. The self-confessed sinner does not have to maintain the appearance of innocence, or to guard himself from contamination by contact with sinners. The knowledge that he is one of their number opens a door to sympathy and eliminates sharpness and cruelty from the judgment made on others.

THE NATURE OF SIN AND FORGIVENESS

Psalm 32:1-5 is based on the premise that unconfessed sin is destructive of human personality. When the psalmist " declared not his sin," his " strength was dried up as by the heat of summer " (Ps. 32:4). Guilt concealed is a wasting disease that erodes and finally destroys life.

Attempts to find a cure for this disease on the psychiatrist's couch may only conceal it under the cover of a " well-adjusted personality," schooled in self-justification. By this method, sin is not dealt with. It is disregarded. Nor can a cure be effected by parading one's sins before those whom the sinner has offended. To do this is to seek forgiveness from those who are unable meaningfully to forgive, and whose forgiveness or continued resentment makes no ultimate difference. The psalmist knows that he must go for forgiveness to him in whom alone cleansing and healing are genuinely to be found.

> I acknowledged my sin to thee,
> and I did not hide my iniquity.
> (V. 5.)

Against this background the first two verses of Ps. 32 are seen to be a statement of that aspect of the divine-human encounter known as " forgiveness." It has a twofold form: the human condition, and God's dealing with that condition. The double pattern is repeated three times in vs. 1 and 2, each repetition having a slightly different emphasis. From v. 5 a middle term may be added to the pattern. It is the human action appropriate to the psalmist's condition. The full expression of the three elements is thus: transgression confessed is met by forgiveness (vs. 1, 5), sin acknowledged is covered (vs. 1, 5), iniquity revealed is not imputed to the guilty party (vs. 2, 5). If the full force of the psalmist's thought is to be appreciated, each of these elements requires elaboration.

Sin as Rebellion. "Transgression" (vs. 1, 5) is a translation of the Hebrew *pésha'*, the most serious Old Testament word for "sin." Its basic meaning is rebellion, and it has the overtones of high treason against the king. The condition of the sinner is thus conceived as that of a willful rebel, who, knowing the responsibilities and duties he bears to his sovereign, nevertheless rejects the sovereign's will in favor of the plans and purposes of his own devising. Wherever transgression is present, the saving relationship between God and man has been broken from the human side.

The action appropriate to rebellion is confession. The entering of a plea of guilty to the charge of treason amounts to admission that one has deserved the death penalty and throws himself on the mercy of the court. This is clearly a more radical act than is normally associated with confession. The admission that on such and such a day I looked lustfully at my neighbor's wife (under the extenuating circumstances that she was making a provocative use of her hips, and that in any event nothing came of it) resembles only remotely the realization that I have forfeited my life by rejection of the authority of God. The first attitude goes only to a single deed, already half excused. The latter admits a radical depravity that has infected and is in control of the total personality.

God's dealing with the condition of rebellion is " forgiveness." He " lifts up " or " carries away " the transgression. In this act he freely and graciously restores the rebel to the status of loyal servant, lifting completely out of the picture both his traitorous disposition and his treasonable acts. In this sense only God can truly forgive. In no human act of forgiveness is the relationship between offender and offended completely restored. The shadow of the offense stands between the two and can never be completely obliterated. The miracle of the grace of God, operative in forgiveness, is that he restores the broken relationship in its totality. The forgiven man is not under suspicion. There remains no presumption that he will be prone to repeat his offense. The act of forgiveness restores fellowship with God without reservation and without prejudice.

Sin as Missing the Mark. In the formula " sin acknowledged and covered," the word descriptive of the human state, *ḥāṭā'* (usually translated " sin "), involves a metaphor from archery. The arrow of will and deed is directed toward a target, and misses. This is the most inclusive Old Testament word for " sin," embracing both unconscious and deliberate violations of the will of God. An archer may shoot wide of the target by no fault of his own, but he may equally be responsible for the miss. A bowstring carelessly allowed to become wet or a hand unsteady from a night's carouse will make the best archer helpless to hit his mark.

Sins done in ignorance were dealt with in Old Testament times by the sacrificial system, which, through its various categories of blood sacrifice, removed the guilt of such sins from the nation. No sacrifice, however potent, was automatically effective for deliberate sins. Missing the mark set before Israel by her God had to be "acknowledged," and full responsibility for it accepted. Such acknowledgment comes much closer to the confession of specific acts contrary to God's will than does acknowledgment of rebellion. What impresses the reader, however, is the psalmist's unreserved openness. God set the target. He missed. He will offer no excuses but will accept the consequences of his failure as his specific responsibility.

God's action in the presence of acknowledged sin is to "cover" it (Hebrew, *kāsāh*), to put it out of sight. As in the case of "forgiveness," the emphasis is on the total elimination of the guilt and the complete restoration of the guilty.

Sin as Distortion. The third statement of the psalmist's theme brings forward a new word for the human condition, '*āwāh* (usually translated "iniquity"), carrying the pictorial meaning of a twisting or turning aside from the road. This word, like "rebellion," points to a total condition of the personality rather than to specific acts of sin. God has set down the right way. For Israel this was defined in terms of the covenant. The individual Israelite found the direction for his life within this covenant. For the Christian the structure of life is given by his fellowship with Christ within the church (the Pauline experience of being "in Christ"). By self-centeredness and self-will, Israelite and Christian alike distort the divine intention. The actual human being is walking by crooked ways of his own devising. The crookedness of his paths with respect to the purpose of God constitutes his "iniquity."

The implication of such words as "rebellion" and "iniquity" is clearly that man is totally depraved, not in the sense that his every thought and deed is evil, but that there is no aspect of his nature free from the intrusion of sin.

God deals with this condition of man by not imputing guilt to the sinner. The complete erasure of the distortion, the total setting right of the wanderer, is again at the center of the psalmist's thought.

The concept of sin found in Ps. 32 begins with the sovereignty of God. Sin is oppressive and destructive because it breaks the relationship between sovereign and subject. In the framework of Old Testament thought, the covenant bond between God and Israel is put in jeopardy by Israel's sin. In the New Testament it is oneness with Jesus Christ that is broken by rebellion. In either case the essence of the matter is human self-deification. Man " sets his heart as the heart of God," declares his autonomy and right to self-determination, and constitutes himself a rebel. To set the record right, man must recognize his true position as traitor and rebel and understand that the only possible deliverance for him is by an act of divine grace, which he in no way deserves but which he most desperately needs.

The author of Ps. 51 supplements the thought of the Thirty-second psalm by adding to it the dimension of renewal, described in poetic language that is unequaled in the devotional literature of any nation.

THE NATURE OF RENEWAL

The presupposition of Ps. 51 is stated in v. 6:

> Behold, thou desirest truth in the inward being;
> therefore teach me wisdom in my secret heart.

The psalmist knows that the heart, the part of his nature concealed from the scrutiny of the world where, in the privacy of his own thoughts, he is most genuinely himself, must be conformed to the character of God and governed by truth and wisdom. Since it is sin in its varied forms that prevents the realization of this inner purity, restoration depends on repentance. The psalmist describes the nature of repentance in three stages (vs. 3, 5).

The sinner must first of all know his transgression. The meaning of the Hebrew verb " know " rules out the kind of casual recognition of sin practiced by many churchgoers who, with undisturbed consciences, agree lightly that " all men are sinners." To " know my transgressions " is to be acutely aware that sin has taken hold in my nature and is ruthlessly destroying me. In the words of the psalmist's explanatory verse, it is to have my sin ever before me (v. 3).

The recognition of the existence of sin in one's own nature must be seconded by an understanding that the injury done to other human beings is a secondary aspect of sin. The primary offense of sin is against the sovereignty of God. It is an abuse of *his* gifts, a degradation of *his* children, an affront to *his* lordship.

> Against thee, thee only, have I sinned,
>   and done that which is evil in thy sight.
>   (V. 4.)

The acknowledgment involved in the first two aspects of repentance must be complete. All claims to merit in the sight of God must be abandoned. This is the meaning of the difficult v. 5:

> Behold, I was brought forth in iniquity,
>   and in sin did my mother conceive me.

The psalmist is not condemning the sexual act as sinful. He is concerned with his own state, not with that of his parents. In a typical Semitic hyperbole he declares that from the time of his birth he was immersed in a world contaminated by rebellion, and that there has been no point in his experience from cradle to grave of which he can say, " Then I was innocent."

From the description of the act of repentance the psalmist goes on to state in the form of a prayer the deliverance he seeks from God (vs. 6-12).

He asks first for cleansing. In the tradition of Jacob (see Chapter V) he anticipates that purification may bring hurt and pain. The Hebrew language has two words for " wash." The first is applied to washing the body, kitchen utensils, and, in general, any object that can be dipped in water or have water poured over it. The second is almost a specific word for washing garments by beating them with a stick or pounding them on a flat rock submerged in water. The psalmist deliberately chooses the second word, rejecting by implication the metaphor of the warm shower and the mild soap pleasantly rinsing away the dirt while the bather luxuriates. He knows that sin is so deeply entrenched in his nature that God may literally have to beat it out of him. The psalmist's meaning is conveyed in a rather inelegant paraphrase of v. 7: Soak me in Clorox, and put me through the Bendix.

Removal of sin, by whatever drastic means, is insufficient unless the source of sin in the human heart is corrected. Again the remedy is drastic. The old heart is too thoroughly habituated to sin to be cleansed. It needs to be replaced, the inner life to be made over by the power of God.

> Create in me a clean heart, O God,
>   and put a new and right spirit within me.
>   (V. 10.)

The operative verb in the first part of the verse is the same word used in the Priestly story of the Creation. The action of God in remaking the human heart is a miracle of his creative power of the same magnitude and wonder as the formation of the universe.

Other Old Testament voices besides that of the Fifty-first Psalm urge the necessity of a remaking of human nature by the power of God. Jeremiah speaks of God in the aftertime putting his law in the nation's heart (Jer. 31:33). Ezekiel looks for the day when God will take away the stony heart and give a heart of flesh (Ezek. 11:19). The New Testament takes up the motif in the story of the encounter between Jesus and Nicodemus (John, ch. 3). Significantly, Jesus is surprised that such a student of the Old Testament as Nicodemus should not be aware of the necessity of a new birth. " Are you a teacher of Israel, and yet you do not understand this? " (John 3:10.)

What was to the Old Testament writers a prayer and a promise, Paul saw fulfilled in the redemptive work of Christ. " If any one is in Christ, he is a new creation." (II Cor. 5:17.)

Although created by the power of God, the new life cannot be left to its own devices to chart its own course and shape its own destiny. This self-determination was the ruin of the old existence. Therefore, the psalmist prays for the continuous presence of God to guide and support him in his restored life. The Holy Spirit, not the human spirit, is to control his existence.

> Take not thy holy Spirit from me. . . .
> Uphold me with a willing spirit.
> (Ps. 51:11-12.)

The writer of the Fifty-first Psalm is an extremist. To a description of total sin and total repentance he adds a prayer for total restoration — old sin purged away, a new life, created by God and sustained by the ministration of his ever-present Spirit. The psalmist proceeds beyond even this to indicate the qualities of the new life for which he prays.

The distinctive characteristic of the new life is joy. The fearfulness and loneliness of his former life are replaced by a profound joy. This is not the effervescent glee of a momentary pleasure, but a permanent quality of life arising from the realization that a miracle, undeserved and unexpected, has been wrought in him by the power of God. His deliverance, his passage from darkness to light, puts a song on his lips and rejoicing in his heart. Accordingly, the new joy appropriate to the renewed heart is properly called " the joy of thy salvation " (v. 12; cf. v. 14).

The psalmist foresees, in addition, that his deliverance has consequences for others as well as for himself. He will become a man with a mission. Others as well as he stand in need of salvation. He will be contrained to share his salvation with them. The heart of the redeemed man is too full to permit him the luxury of silence. He must teach others the new meaning that life has acquired for him and turn men toward the God of salvation (vs. 13-14). The missionary motive appears in Ps. 51, as in the New Testament, as the inescapable consequence of salvation.

THE PILGRIMAGE OF A SOUL

In Ps. 73 the thought of Ps. 32 and 51 is incarnated in the life experience of a man. This psalm is redemption recollected in tranquillity. Its writer was not a wicked man by the gross standard of theft or murder. His temptation and sin are of the subtler form that preys upon the conscientious and the good. This unique autobiographical psalm allows us to see salvation at work among those who apparently stand nearest to God, and in this respect it invites comparison with Jesus' parable of the elder brother (Luke 15:25-32).

The text of Ps. 73 indicates that its author was a priest, a teacher of religion at a time when the religion of Israel was to some degree proscribed and its adherents under persecution. He had taught and believed that God rewards his faithful servants with prosperity and well-being. " Truly God is good to the upright." (V. 1.) But the facts of his world denied his theology. The wicked prospered. (V. 3.) They were free of pain and trouble. (V. 4.) Their bellies were sleek and their eyes bulging with luxurious living. (V. 7.) They mocked at any threat of divine judgment, and their arrogance protected them from reprisal by human justice. (Vs. 11, 6.) Far from being repelled by their cruelty, the people applauded them for vigor and aggressiveness. (V. 10.) The psalmist's own position was precisely the opposite. He had been scrupulous in his obedience to the moral and ritual demands of his religion, and his piety had gained him nothing but sneers and hard knocks. (V. 14.)

The disparity between belief and reality led the psalmist to doubt his faith, and to call in question the goodness of God. (V. 2.) His first reaction to his rising resentment was to use his teaching office to communicate his doubt to others. He would tell the people that their religion was a gigantic hoax, piety and obedience to God a futile waste of time. If they wished to prosper in the world, let them imitate the proud and arrogant, for concerning the deeds of men God neither knows nor cares. (V. 15; cf. v. 11.)

He was dissuaded from this course by concern for the people to whom he would be speaking. He had nothing to offer them but his frustration. What he would say would be a patchwork of negatives, destructive of the moral structure of society, contributing nothing to the people's need, but plunging them into the same morass of doubt as himself.

The conscience of the teacher consists in this. He must remain true " to the generation of God's children " (v. 15). The sophisticated agnostic, whether in the pulpit or the university, often delights in destroying, in the name of honesty, the beliefs on which his hearers naïvely rely. It may be good sport to see the freshmen squirm as their cherished convictions are exploded by the dynamite of irresistible logic. But unless the teacher can replace the shattered beliefs by a more substantial structure than a dog-eat-dog existence, governed by the rule of " winner takes all," he had better leave the hearers their faith, and look to the repair of his own.

The psalmist, rejecting a public proclamation of his frustration, decided to think the problem through to a solution (v. 16). Western man has a blind faith in this process, and " thinking it through " is very nearly a religion. It is so much the better if the procedure can be reinforced by group discussion. The problems of life are solved by bringing in an expert speaker, breaking up into " buzz sessions," and coming together afterward to report the findings.

As the psalmist discovered, the thinking processes are under a decisive handicap. They require an atmosphere of calm detachment for their most efficient functioning. However, when a problem is pressing hard on the life of a person, the pressure of his emotions immobilizes his thought. A father whose son has just died in an accident cannot think dispassionately on the problem of pain and death. Similarly, the psalmist, tormented by the collapse of his basic convictions under the stress of events, found himself incapable of logic. " It was too painful for me." (V. 16, KJV.)

What course remained open to the psalmist? The characteristic Biblical way of facing a problem is to take it into the presence of God. This was how Habakkuk attempted to find an explanation of why the Chaldeans were allowed to exercise their cruelty on the defeated Israelites. His formulation is a classic expression of the prophetic "method" of dealing with crucial problems.

> I will take my stand to watch,
>   and station myself on the tower,
> and look forth to see what he [i.e., God] will say
>   to me.
>
> (Hab. 2:1.)

The attitude of the prophet is misrepresented if viewed either as a technique in problem-solving or as a passing off of responsibility to God. If it is true, as the Biblical revelation insists, that the meaning of life is given in an encounter with God, it follows that the problems of life must be met and solved in the same context. When a man follows the psalmist "into the sanctuary of God" (Ps. 73:17), he does not check his brains at the door and enter as a subhuman receptacle into which God will pour "the solution." He comes in his full humanity, and in the mystery of the God-man relationship he seeks and finds illumination, never totally satisfying but sufficient to enable him to overcome his problem, or at least to live with it.

Not infrequently, as in the case of the psalmist, the situation is seen in a different light in the sanctuary from that in which it appears in the world. The psalmist felt that the difficulty was in his surroundings. In the sanctuary he learned that it was in himself.

The answer of the psalmist to the problem of the prosperity of the wicked is meager enough. Their ascendancy is temporary. Their situation, maintained by violence, is precarious. They may at one moment enjoy the full bloom of success and the next be plunged to destruction. This " slippery " quality of trust in wealth or power is a commonplace of prophetic preaching (see p. 151), and by itself it could hardly answer the psalmist's doubt of the goodness of God.

The sanctuary experience forced the psalmist to examine himself. When he did so, he discovered a radical self-centeredness. The motive of his protest had been envy (v. 3). The wicked were better off than he, enjoying what should have been his by right of superior piety. He had wanted from life the same things as the oppressors: a full stomach, rich garments, a gold chain around his neck, and the plaudits of the crowd in his ears. In this, he says, " I was like a beast toward thee " (v. 22), content with the satisfaction of the needs that he shared with the animals, and seeing life in essentially animal terms.

In the sanctuary, the center of the psalmist's life was changed from self to God. He ceased to make the mistake of Cain (see p. 88) and to compare himself on the horizontal level with his neighbors. He now saw himself, not as a man in a cruel and unjust world, but as a man in the presence of God.

The change of center made possible a startling revelation. In his poverty and oppression, he nevertheless possessed the only thing in the world worth having: the presence of God in his life (v. 23). To be with God, to have his guidance and counsel, and to be the heir of his promises (v. 24) is a treasure beside which the possessions of the worldly are shoddy trinkets. If he could gain the latter by the loss of the former, he would be throwing away everything in return for a phantom (v. 20). The prosperity of the wicked was a dream, the presence of God was the reality.

On this point Paul and the psalmist are in close, almost verbal, agreement.

> Whom have I in heaven but thee?
>> And there is nothing upon earth that I desire
>> besides thee.
>>
>> (V. 25.)

This corresponds to Paul's "I decided to know nothing among you except Jesus Christ and him crucified" (I Cor. 2:2). Paul's "Though our outer nature is wasting away, our inner nature is being renewed every day" (II Cor. 4:16) echoes the psalmist's

> My heart and my flesh may fail,
>> but God is the strength of my life and my
>> portion for ever
>>
>> (Ps. 73:26).

Psalm 73 allows us to see what redemption and salvation essentially are. They involve a shift in the center of life from self to God, a change that means a thoroughgoing reorganization of every element of life to such a degree that the life which emerges is new — all its values, motives, ideas, and perspectives transformed.

The autobiography of the psalmist provides the right note on which to close this discussion of the place of the Old Testament in Christian preaching. The Christian preacher is the witness and herald of the revolutionary redemptive work of God in Jesus Christ. His message is the transformation, unlimited in its range and uncontrollable in its results, wrought in human existence by God in Christ. Governed by this basic task, he comes to the Old Testament. He cannot identify himself completely with the revelation he finds there, but its pages enable him to see more clearly the nature of sin as self-centeredness and self-deification. The promise of redemption, which for Israel was always hidden just beyond the horizon, allows him to see more clearly its fulfillment in the gospel. The nature of the relationship between God and man, the peculiar quality of forgiveness, faith, and the new life, become clearer to him through the inspired struggle of the old order to realize them in its life. Thus the Old Testament adds a dimension of richness and depth to Christian preaching which would be impossible in its absence. The church does not preach the Old Testament, but it can, to its own great good, embrace the Old Testament *within* its preaching.

Index

□ THE
OLD TESTAMENT IN CHRISTIAN PREACHING □

By Lawrence E. Toombs

This book is written for the specific purpose of indicating to the parish minister the significance which modern Old Testament studies possess for the preaching of the gospel. An enormous amount of fruitful work has been done on the Old Testament in recent years, but a serious gap exists between the results of this work and the presentation of these results in the pulpits of the churches. A loss is sustained when so much of really great potential preaching value is left unused.

Dr. Toombs, who is an authority on the Old Testament, devotes his first chapter to an examination of the relationship between the Old and the New Testaments and of the implications that an understanding of this relationship has for the preacher's task. Attention is given to the bearing of archaeological, historical, and critical studies on the interpretation of the Old Testament, but the whole work is dominated by the question: Can Old Testament themes properly be used in Christian preaching?

For answer Dr. Toombs presents no generalized rationale. On the contrary, he points to literally hundreds of specific Old Testament passages from which the Christian preacher can draw pertinent moral and doctrinal lessons. Notable among these passages are the story of the Fall, the drunkenness of Noah, the sacrifice of Isaac, the conversion of Jacob. Perhaps the closeness